Routledge Revivals

The Twelfth Hour of Capitalism

The Twelfth Hour of Capitalism

by

Kuno Renatus

Translated from the German by
E. W. Dickes

Routledge Revivals
Routledge
Taylor & Francis Group

First published in 1932 by Alfred A. Knopf, Inc.

This edition first published in 2019 by Routledge
2 Park Square, Milton Park, Abingdon, Oxon, OX14 4RN
and by Routledge
52 Vanderbilt Avenue, New York, NY 10017, USA

Routledge is an imprint of the Taylor & Francis Group, an informa business

Publisher's Note
The publisher has gone to great lengths to ensure the quality of this reprint but points out that some imperfections in the original copies may be apparent.

Disclaimer
The publisher has made every effort to trace copyright holders and welcomes correspondence from those they have been unable to contact.

A Library of Congress record exists under ISBN:

ISBN 13: 978-0-367-24554-2 (hbk)
ISBN 13: 978-0-367-24562-7 (pbk)
ISBN 13: 978-0-429-28315-4 (ebk)

THE TWELFTH HOUR OF CAPITALISM

THE TWELFTH HOUR OF CAPITALISM

BY KUNO RENATUS

TRANSLATED FROM THE GERMAN BY

E. W. DICKES

MCM XXXII

ALFRED · A · KNOPF · NEW YORK

First Edition

PUBLISHED IN GERMANY UNDER THE TITLE
DIE ZWÖLFTE STUNDE DER WELTWIRTSCHAFT
(C. H. BECK'SCHE VERLAGSBUCHHANDLUNG, MUNICH)
FIRST PUBLISHED IN ENGLISH IN 1932

Manufactured in the United States of America

"Unless all the signs are deceiving us, we are living in a period in which, if the existing system of trade and industry is to be preserved from grave and lasting convulsions, it is necessary to introduce a broader and more generous conception of the idea of capital."

DR. BRÜNING, GERMAN CHANCELLOR,
IN HIS SPEECH OF JUNE 27, 1931

PREFACE

To the English Edition

In the months that have passed since the appearance of the German original of this book, nothing has happened to upset the interpretation given by the author to the world economic crisis—gladly as he would have seen himself put in the wrong by a revival of trade. International unemployment has further increased—in Germany the number of the workless has risen above six millions, in France it has reached one million—and the general picture here given is in no way invalidated by the fact that in Britain, under the working of the new currency policy, unemployment has slightly fallen. The essential point is that the general volume of world trade has further decreased.

Of the events that have happened since the book was finished, two are particularly relevant to its train of thought. Britain has definitely broken with the tradition of free trade which lifted her up in the nineteenth century to a position of unparalleled power. This change of system is the necessary consequence of the abandonment of the gold standard. It is impossible to praise too highly the British national discipline which so far has prevented the sharp fall of sterling on the international market from producing the slightest trace of inflation within the country. Little as an Englishman may now regret the going off gold as an emergency measure, there are few Englishmen who do not hope and expect to find the gold standard restored at some time, on a basis still to be found. Only when that stage has been reached will it be perfectly plain what it was essentially that made the abandonment of gold necessary, and drove the country into it: the great reduction which was thus effected in British indebtedness, measured, not by the present internal purchasing power of the paper pound, but by the international standard of gold. Although, owing to the unchanged internal purchasing power, the reduction has as yet worked itself out only partially, it has already brought manifest relief to the country's economic situation, and the British nation appreciates the relief. Will it recognize the deeper causes of this relief, will it realize that they do not lie simply in the cutting off of the Empire from the outer world (a step which is in conflict with the tradition of British history), but in the reduction of indebtedness? And will that fact reveal to it the direction in which the path to real recovery lies?

In the United States President Hoover has issued an appeal against bank-note-hoarding. We drew attention in the last chapter of this book to the American hoarding, which has since grown to the dimensions of a menacing calamity. President Hoover estimates the amount of hoarded notes at 1,300,000,000 dollars. What a mass of mistrust finds expression in such a figure, and what an extent of unremunerative burdening of the note bank! If one takes the number of the workless in America as ten millions, there are 130 dollars withheld from employment for every workless person! But experience has shown that in matters of this sort purely moral appeals are rarely effective. The figure serves more as an indication for everyone of the caution which his neighbour is showing in dealing with his money, and everyone asks himself: "If he is being cautious, can I be less so?" Already the United States Government has taken a further step and gone to work with much more substantial means than those of a mere appeal. Under Senator Glass's Bill the note cover is being slightly reduced. The American position is strong enough to enable this change in the stipulated cover (at present proposed for one year only) to be made without any immediate danger to the dollar. As the number of notes in circulation is being increased, it is quite likely that some of the hoarded notes will also come back into use. But it must not be overlooked that the step is a symptom of America's expectation of further withdrawals of gold by France (the total gold shipped by America in January 1932 is estimated at some 112,000,000 dollars), and of her desire to ease her position in regard to France. This may bring temporary assistance to American trade and industry, but it is the very reverse of the way back to the general prosperity of the past; it is, on the contrary, a further move towards independence of the world outside and so a step away from the unity of the world's economic system.

Meanwhile, little Switzerland has issued a 3.5 per cent federal loan, a type of loan which has been absent for decades from the Swiss Stock Exchange List. This course is indicated by the trend of the market; when will the Governments of the great creditor States systematically embark on it and push on with it, and so put a term to the sufferings of the nations?

KUNO RENATUS

February 1932

CONTENTS

CONTENTS

Chapter One

THE TASK

President Hoover's Message [of June 20, 1931, to the Governments concerned] introduced a new stage in the treatment of the international indebtedness. The changed situation demands fresh thinking. The purpose of this book is to offer a contribution to this thinking.

At the same time we are well aware that it would be a great mistake to exaggerate the finality of the change in the American attitude. There is no guarantee yet that America may not brusquely revert any day to her earlier standpoint of the creditor concerned simply for his dues. The repercussions of Mr. Hoover's second move, in October 1931, showed plainly enough how strongly the Senators object to a prolongation of the moratorium. Can we be sure that the coming Presidential elections will not be dominated by the slogan: "Not a cent off Europe's debts; give the whole lot to the farmers"? However, in spite of all the pessimists who are already announcing that Hoover is "done for," there remains one indisputable gain from Mr. Hoover's action, in the fact that the American Government has subordinated the question of the public debts to that of the private credits.

It is from this point that we have to think things out.

ALL THE WORLD AT A LOSS

Be it admitted, however, to begin with, that the world was never so entirely at a loss as in these days. Undoubtedly men have many times been in more desperate straits—when, for instance, the Black Death was striding across the Continent, and the Flagellants, appealing in penitence to an angered God beyond the clouds, sought to placate him by self-inflicted tortures. For all that, in the midst of their despair these men were sure of one thing—that the pains they had to endure were a visitation brought on them by their own sinfulness. The men of today do not know why they are suffering. Never before has it happened in the history of Western civilization that the crops rotted in the silos while the unemployed went hungry; that the oil-wells were laid idle by the Government and had to be protected by that same Government's soldiery from the fury of the population for whose benefit the stoppage was ordered; that the American Farm Board had no more hopeful advice to offer the farmers than that they should plough up every third furrow in the cotton fields.

Meanwhile there are ships enough lying idle in the ports, waiting for a chance to bring the surplus to the destitute; there are sailors enough waiting to sign on and get in the cargoes; there is capital enough out of use and waiting for the chance to put the raw material to good account. Yet it is proving impossible to bridge the gulf between the goods and those who need them. What ever has happened?

Technical progress has banished from human memory the regional famines which carried men off in past centuries when the harvests failed, only to substitute for them the new famine of world-wide unemployment. And yet the apparatus of production was never at such a pitch of perfection as now, the means of transport never more efficient, the technique of credit never more thoroughly adjusted to a delicate responsiveness. Nor was the realization of responsibility towards the working masses ever more thorough—at least on paper. No one would dare today to proclaim, with the cynicism of a Ricardo, that there is no economic purpose to be served by trying to help the poor. Never before was there an International Labour Office in existence, and never was the number of workless in the world greater. What ever has happened?

This state of things is being accepted with a strange fatalism. What has become of the prophesyings of all the economic experts, who forecast for us from quarter to quarter the coming revival of trade? No one dares to prophesy any longer. The German semiofficial Institut für Konjunkturforschung, that meteorological observatory for the country's trade, wrote in its report of April 1, 1931: "The process of liquidation of the depression is approaching its conclusion. The realization of this encourages the hope that the depression will discharge itself before very long into a new revival. It may, therefore, be opportune to set down some observations in regard . . . to the limitations of the coming revival." And as lately as May 13 this institution announced that "speaking generally, the downward movement in trade is plainly coming to a stop." In the report for the week ending August 26, however, the institution expressly forbore from attempting any further prognosis of future developments in regard to unemployment.

People are seeking comfort in the reflection that things were much the same after the Napoleonic wars, and are preparing themselves for a trial of endurance. We are all sitting waiting in Noah's ark, while the rain pours down incessantly outside; but no dove comes in, and we scarcely venture any longer to put our hands out of the window now and again—it is plainly raining still as hard as ever.

But we must not go on with this fatalistic acceptance of things. We must determine at least to find out what is happening. So surely as man is distinguished from the beast by the longer nose that enables him to probe a mystery, so surely are we entitled to declare that we mean to find out what is up. If we are doomed to destruction, let us at least learn the why and the wherefore of our ruin.

TIME PRESSING

In this world-at-a-loss, then, there is one separate tangible collection of data, the complex of Reparations. What is the economic significance of the Reparation payments?

The situation at the moment is that everyone in Germany knows that at the end of the Hoover year no Reparations can possibly be paid. On the other hand, the more their own troubles mount up through the general crisis, the less are the creditor States in a position to dispense with the revenues which the German payments represent in their national budgets.

So the unity of the close-knit complex of world economic relations is threatening to burst asunder at this point: Germany, hard pressed by her troubles, is no longer able to pay; the rest, hard pressed by their own, cannot forgo payment; or at least do not believe that they can.

And now the dramatic question arises: Are there two separate forces, Reparations on one side, the crisis in world trade on the other, that between them are sundering the economic unity of the world? Or can it be one and the same force that is blasting the world under two outward forms? Or, finally, is there at least some sort of interdependence between the two, and if so, what is its nature?

The scheme of Reparation payments was drawn up under the pressure of the victor, who wanted his money back just as a private person would want to see again at some time or other the money he has lent out. The British suggestion simply to write off all war debts (expressly reiterated in the Balfour Note of August 1, 1922) was rejected by the United States. The suggestion of the American universities themselves (manifesto of the Faculty of Political Science of Columbia University, New York, December 19, 1926; statement of Princeton University, New Jersey, March 10, 1927) that the war debts should be written off was similarly met with a flat refusal by the American Government (Mr. Mellon's reply of March 15, 1927). The simple logic of the situation held the field: "We lent the money and we want it back." Not for a moment was any thought given to the effect of the payments on world trade. The only concern shown was with the question whether Germany was likely to be in a position to bear her burdens. That question was left to the test of practical experience.

For the rest, it was, of course, taken as axiomatic that the payments would enrich the creditor powers in proportion as they impoverished Germany. And, taken at its face value, that expectation has been fulfilled to the letter: the gold of the Reichsbank has travelled to the vaults of the American Federal Reserve Bank and the Bank of France. In actual fact, however, the economic situation of the creditor countries has become decidedly worse since the commencement of the full annuities. Over against the gains to the State budgets from the receipt of the Reparation payments, there stand business losses many times greater, suffered by the trade and industry of the creditor countries through falling prices, reduced values of securities, and so on, and these in turn have resulted in diminutions of revenue from taxation and customs duties.

Is there any intimate connexion between these circumstances, or is it simply through the "cussedness" of things that Reparations only began to flow in in full volume just at the moment when the world crisis broke out?

The average German will have a ready and unhesitating answer. He quite rightly looks at the thing from his own, the German, point of view, and he knows, from its actual pressure, just where the shoe pinches. He has not the slightest shadow of doubt that there is a connexion between Reparations and these economic troubles. If we had not had to pay Reparations, if the money had remained in the country, things would now be going very much better with us. Ergo, let us have an end of the payments, and the soonest possible. That line of argument seems unanswerable, and its appeal is the strength of the extreme parties.

For the majority, however, of the trained economists that view is just childish. They see no connexion whatever between Reparations and the crisis in world trade and industry. They had waited in genuine faith for the great revival in trade that was to follow the acceptance of the Young Plan. The failure of the revival to come, the coincidence of the beginning of the normal Reparation year with the outbreak of the world crisis, is, in their eyes, merely an unhappy chance, unconnected with any automatic repercussion.

As an example of this line of argument we may quote the words of one of the most gifted of the German liberal economists. On August 17, 1930 Richard Lewinsohn wrote in the *Vossische Zeitung*: "The world economic crisis proceeds from quite different causes, and it would require a very arbitrary assumption of interconnexions to enable any substantial part of the crisis to be attributed to the Dawes Plan or the Young Plan. The good results which would undoubtedly have come from the final clearing up of the plan of Reparations have been swamped by the outbreak of the great international economic crisis."

The view here expressed is also universally held abroad. It is pointed out especially, as disposing of any connexion between the crisis and the Reparation payments, that the effects of the crisis are on an altogether different scale from those of the relatively trifling Reparation payments. A typical expression of this view has been given by Mr. Houghton: when the debtors, he said, were paying out twelve milliards of dollars a year, it was inconceivable that the few hundred million dollars which went to America could be a bar to the debtors' prosperity. The logic of this seems incontrovertible. But if this contention, that Reparations and the world crisis have no causal connexion whatever with each other, is correct, it follows at once that: there is no reason to expect any relief from the world crisis if the Reparation payments are dispensed with. In that case, a total or partial remission of Reparations is an act of brotherly love for the poor hungry Germans and, further, perhaps an act of political wisdom, preserving the most populous country in central Europe from Bolshevism; but as a means of reviving world trade there is nothing to be expected from it.

Does not this conclusion seem to be confirmed already by the "failure" of Mr. Hoover's action? The revival of trade which was confidently anticipated as a result of the announcement of the year's moratorium for Reparations and war debts has not come to the expected extent. It is true that things would be looking much worse in the world today if the year's moratorium had not been declared; but to ask people to realize that is to put too heavy a strain on their imagination.

If, however, the soundness of this argument is admitted, we Germans have nothing left to hope for. We must be quite clear as to that. Hoover did not issue his Message out of any sentimental affection for the Germans. He issued it under the pressure of the distress in the Western States, and as a last attempt to save his laurels as the Prosperity President. So far as he personally was concerned, he had long been clinging obstinately to the standpoint that the world depression was no argument for a revision of world debts. His sudden volte-face was an empirical experiment, born of the pressure of necessity. It effected for the first time before all the world a linking of the world crisis with world indebtedness; but only empirically, and only experimentally. No change of theoretical judgment can be assumed in explanation of Mr. Hoover's change of front; quite the contrary. In his Message Mr. Hoover expressly declared that the payments under the Young Plan would be "supportable in normal times." No admission here of any interreaction between crisis and payments: the plan is all right, only the times are "abnormal."

But suppose the experiment fails? Suppose the world depression does not react as expected to the postponement of payment? In that case Mr. Houghton's logic is adhered to.

A much more radical repudiation of all connexion between crisis and Reparations has been published by the *Temps*. That organ performs the feat of arguing out of existence even the connexion between Reparation payments and Germany's own crisis. After the Basel report became public property, it wrote: "Since 1924 Germany has taken up eighteen milliards of foreign credits; in the same period she has paid only some ten milliards in Reparations. This clearly proves that Germany has not yet made any Reparation payment out of her own resources. So much the more perverse is the contention that Reparations are the cause of Germany's financial crisis." And it would be quite a mistake to suppose that this train of reasoning on the part of the gravest of the French newspapers is meant as a joke.

Enough of such curiosities. The key to the world's economic welfare is today in America's hands. And the attitude that the very best Americans would take up today towards any attempt at a fresh settlement of the complex of debts is, perhaps, best illustrated by the statement made by Mr. Silas Strawn, the leader of the American delegation at the Washington session of the International Chamber of Commerce; he demanded that good grounds should first be shown on which to convince a hundred million Americans that they must saddle themselves with eleven milliards of dollars on top of all the rest. The people at home, he said, were finding their present taxes quite enough.

No one has yet supplied these good grounds to the Americans. Germany's troubles are certainly no such good grounds. Much as has already been written about Reparations, no one has yet taken on himself the task of thinking out, step by step, the economic fate of the payments made and their influence on world trade.

If, however, these good grounds are not supplied, there is a great danger that on the day of the American Presidential election the American voters, who see in the loss of the payments simply an increase in their burden of taxation, will make short work of Mr. Hoover's good intentions.

THE INQUIRY DEFINED

Clearly it is high time that there should be some hard thinking on the questions:

What relationship is there between Reparations and the world crisis? Is the coincidence of the outbreak of the crisis with the coming of the Dawes Plan into full operation mere chance, or is there some connexion between the two events?

This inquiry raises the question of the relations between two incommensurable unknowns.

Reparations themselves are only a "dependent variable," the outward expression of a circumstance that goes much deeper, the world indebtedness produced by the War. We shall be driven very early in our inquiry to leave "Reparations" alone, to dig down to the root cause, and to substitute for them "world indebtedness."

The world crisis, on the other hand, is a complex phenomenon. The only direct data that we have to begin with are the symptoms of the crisis, the facts of falling trade. The "crisis" itself is a conception burdened in advance with all conceivable interpretations and theories. The result is that in our publicist-ridden century scarcely any element of the crisis can be mentioned without arousing the impulse to explain it away in the reader. Every single fact of the crisis carries with it already its theory-in-occupation.

If we are to see clearly in the midst of this confusion, there is nothing for it but to consider separately each of the two groups of facts the nature of whose interconnexion we are out to investigate, and to proceed from each separate group in our search for its particular sources of entanglement with the other. We shall accordingly inquire, entirely independently of each other, into these two questions:

1. What are the causes of the world crisis in trade and industry?

2. What are the effects on world trade and industry of the Reparation payments or of the world indebtedness?

We shall proceed, then, to trace from each of the two unknowns the course of its ascertained associations. We shall see the series of causes to which we shall be referred back when we start from the facts of the crisis, and the series of effects to which we shall be referred forward when we start from the facts of the world indebtedness and the payments made for its service. We shall be greatly interested to discover whether the two series, that of causes and that of effects, will intersect at any point.

Only by keeping clean apart in this way the things into whose possible interconnexion we are inquiring can we hope to carry conviction in presenting the results of our inquiry. For a crisis—we are well aware of it—is so complex a thing, its economic ramifications are so widespread, that not a great deal of dialectical ingenuity would be needed to smuggle in among its branching roots some cause quite foreign to it. We should not be surprised if critically minded readers approach our demonstration armed in advance with scepticism. Only a clean cut, severing all that is irrelevant, will enable us to convince them.

THINKING IN TERMS OF WORLD TRADE

Another thing is necessary: we must raise ourselves above a merely German outlook and think in terms of the world's trade and industry. It is very human to love one's country, but we must not for a moment be led into national particularism. Most certainly it is useless to raise the cry of Germany's distressful state. If that were of any service, it could not but have served long ago. We Germans are thoroughly used to the great decisions in the history of Western civilization taking place over our prostrate bodies. For seventeen years now, no people in the world has been so continuously maltreated by Fate as the German people. A whole generation has now grown up that no longer knows what a secure existence is, that knows only precariousness. How much that means to a nation's spirit, what potentialities of explosion have in this way been accumulated, is more than the other nations can have any notion of. We Germans have to suffer most from the crisis; so much is a settled matter. The other nations will not be excessively impressed, however much statistical material we may bring forward to prove the fact. Number one still comes first with everybody. We Germans are almost back again in much the same situation as during the War: the complainings of the other capitalist countries remind us rather of the war-time plaint of our neutral neighbours in their sore distress at the necessity of keeping their armies—at the base. The competition in complaint, each regarding himself as the hardest hit, can at best only lead to each nation withdrawing into itself. And the only thing that can help Germany is the world-wide extent of the crisis, the fact that the fate of the whole world is bound up with that of Germany.

Let no one jump to the conclusion that with the dawning recognition of this world-wide interdependence we shall be helped over all the stiles that remain. It has become almost the last remaining rag of pride of the German newspaper-reading man-in-the-suburb that the economic world cannot manage without Germany, that her troubles are involving all the other countries, and so on.

However, so long as this fact of interdependence exists, it is our duty to make it the starting-point of our consideration; if only because it is the Thing that Is and the thing that has hitherto provided us with our sustenance. To abandon it prematurely, as our advocates of self-sufficiency propose, because the unity of world trade seems today to be becoming precarious, would be to sever with our own hand the ropes that might be the saving of Germany. Self-sufficiency may be a wonderful recipe for the great capitalist countries with wide colonial possessions, which can comparatively easily close their doors to the outer world. That, no doubt, is why the word is nowhere so loudly bawled as in Germany.

NO IDEOLOGY-MONGERING

We must avoid a narrow outlook from a purely German standpoint; we want equally to avoid the opposite error, that of losing touch with the world in a strato-sphere of ideologies. We shall tie ourselves down rigorously to the soil of the existing economic system. To reply to the question what has brought about the world crisis by peppering the whole economic system with negative signs and proclaiming the "end of capitalism" seems to us too simple. It is just as unhelpful as if a man were to go to the dentist and ask what is the matter with his aching tooth, and the dentist, without even looking inside the man's mouth, were to reply: "What do you expect, my dear sir? Don't you know that among all the members of civilized humanity today the jaws have degenerated? You must give up your tooth as a bad job. You must entirely change the whole system, you must go over to the rational jaw of artificial teeth." Prophets of that sort abound today. And the comparison is much too kind to them, for the dentists have behind them a generation of experience with sets of teeth; while the economic systems urged on us as alternatives to the capitalist system, whether they go by the name of Economic Planning or Self-sufficiency, are as yet no more than fictions of the intelligence, or have been tried only under conditions which are not comparable with those of German trade and industry.

For the present we have still our own teeth in our heads, and they have enabled us to eat so far, and if they are undoubtedly bad, and hurting a great deal, they are at least the teeth we have grown up with and got used to. It is just that that needs to be said to the Romanticists among the economic prophets: If there is one thing that is indubitable, it is that the capitalist system "just growed," it was never built up on a preconceived plan. It was complete long before the word "capitalism" was invented by any man. (Who, by the way, did invent it?) When Adam Smith began to write, the industrial division of labour had long been put into practice. We do not mean to argue that everything that is is for the best. But we believe only in the self-correction or self-negation of capitalism, proceeding from capitalism itself—and that has, indeed, been carried no little distance already and is daily being carried further. These tendencies need to be invested with conscious direction, not interpreted as a signal for the demolition of the whole system on the ground that it is already going to rack and ruin.

So much has been said by way of a prefatory dismissal of the irrelevant. That whole complex of ideas belongs to the category of general inferences, which each reader is at liberty to draw for himself, and has no place in our inquiry. Our purpose is to discover how the facts hang together, and to leave it at that. We shall carry out our inquiry without grinding ideological axes and without sentimental rhetoric. For we Germans have no weapon left but logic.

Chapter Two

THE FACTS

The symptoms of the crisis have so often been recounted—and every issue of the newspapers has new ones to report—that it is out of the question to enumerate them all here. We will only recall the various classes of symptoms and note the multiplicity of the series of facts in which the crisis is being manifested. For any satisfactory theory of the crisis must take account as far as possible of all its symptoms. On the other hand, we shall view suspiciously any explanation which fits only one group of facts, and needs modification for every phenomenon outside that group.

The main groups of symptoms are: (1) unemployment; (2) the fall in prices; (3) the decline in production, the shrinkage of the whole volume of trade, and in connexion therewith the fall in the quotations for stock-exchange securities; (4) the fall in the international discount rates, money lying fallow while long-term credits grow dearer.

UNEMPLOYMENT

The figures of world unemployment have so often been published that there is no need for us to repeat them here in detail. Suffice it to quote the total figure: today at least twenty to twenty-two million persons are unemployed in the world, a people of about the size of the population of Spain. That does not include their dependants. Adding the dependants, we arrive at roughly four times as many, or a people more numerous than any European nation, living today within the economic system of our world, but unable to find either work or support by work.

Unemployment on this scale is a thing unprecedented. During the severest crises of the nineteenth century not only the absolute but the relative numbers of unemployed were far below the present figure. It has, especially, never before happened that countries in every continent and of the most diverse economic character, industrial and agricultural countries alike, those with a long past of capitalist development and colonial countries only now being opened up, were so uniformly in the throes of acute unemployment. Formerly that malady was confined more or less to the centre in which it broke out or to neighbouring centres—for instance, to the highly industrialized countries. This time the picture is very different. It is as if a bacillus had attacked the whole world.

On the other hand, the degree or intensity of world unemployment shows remarkable geographical variations. The crisis originated, of course, this time in Germany, and we have all been used for a long time past to seeing Germany holding, in percentage of population, the unwelcome distinction of record unemployment. People no longer think about it; it is as if Germany had a start, and it is not so easy for the other countries to catch up with her. What would be the use of paying much attention to it? Is it not, after all, only natural that in Germany, the conquered country, whose trade and industry have been the most cruelly denuded of capital, the degree of unemployment should be the worst? The same considerations make it seem only natural that Austria, herself a conquered and impoverished country, should be not far behind Germany in degree of unemployment: in Germany at the end of March 1931, 7.7 per cent of the population were unemployed, in Austria 5.1 per cent. But then we suddenly find to our astonishment that the victorious United States, the country with the most capital in the world, has a worse degree of unemployment than poor Austria, actually coming next after Germany: in March 1931 she had 7,500,000 unemployed, equivalent to 6.1 per cent of the population, and bringing her next after Germany; and if the latest estimates of American unemployment, running into nine and ten millions, are correct, the United States has an excellent chance of beating Germany's record. It is not surprising to find Britain not much better off, with an unmistakable crisis of her own, but she is well behind Germany and the United States, coming third, with 5.5 per cent of the population unemployed at the end of March 1931.

The reply may seem tempting that Germany, Britain, and America are the three principal industrial countries. But France has certainly a very respectable industry, and yet her unemployment figure was not even one per cent (0.9 per cent at the end of March 1931). This French oasis of employment has often enough been the subject of wonderment. It is usually explained by reference to certain features of the French "national character," the lower level of the wages of the French worker, and so on. Most of these are the very factors which used to be referred to in explanation of France's backwardness in industry. For the rest, German opinion is comforted by the unexpressed conviction that unemployment will soon go up in France as well.

The Scandinavian countries were also long regarded as secure oases of employment. Now, however, we are presented with the picture of Denmark, an almost entirely agricultural country, one which was not directly affected by the War, and one with an extremely well-organized economic life, suffering from double the French unemployment percentage—2 per cent.

We have thus the following very remarkable facts: Unemployment has spread over the whole world; scarcely a country is immune from it. But it is very unequally distributed. It varies widely—7 to 8 per cent in Germany and America; 0.1 per cent in Jugoslavia. If one thinks of the relative level of unemployment in terms of heights on the face of the earth, one gets a very remarkable relief map of unemployment.

For the distribution of levels on this relief map does not depend on whether a country is industrial or agricultural, a victor country or vanquished, a country rich in capital or poor. On what in the world, then, does it depend? No economist has yet succeeded in answering that question.

It seems to the writer, however, that the customary expression of relative unemployment in percentages of the population is inadequate and liable to lead to wrong conclusions. Unemployed persons are persons who formerly were in employment; thus, the greater the percentage of employed persons in relation to the population of a country, the greater will be the percentage of unemployed to be expected when a world depression comes. If one regards the relative distribution of unemployment from this point of view, one finds at once that Germany has the greatest number of employed persons—namely, 51.3 per cent of the population. The United States, on the contrary, popularly regarded among us as the country in which everybody, the richest and the poorest alike, is on the hunt for the dollar and dies in the harness of some paid job, showed only 39.4 per cent of employed persons in the census of 1920. Had the United States as high a percentage as Germany of employed persons, how heavy, one sees at once, would be its percentage of unemployed now.

Still more surprising is the result at which we arrive if we measure German unemployment by the pre-war standard, which we still more or less consciously regard as a sort of normal economic standard, because at that time, even without the assistance of the social welfare apparatus, pretty well everyone was sure of his daily bread. At the last census of employment before the War in Germany (June 12, 1907), the number of employed persons, corrected for the present area of German territory, was 25,100,000, or 45.7 per cent of the population (taking the population at that date, corrected for the present area, as 55,000,000). Thus, even in 1907, in the Germany that today has for us the charm of a pre-war idyll, the percentage of employed persons was much higher than in the America of today, which we seem to see surrounded by a halo of industry.

Yet further, considering Germany only: the present crisis has not yet driven out of German economic life through unemployment as many persons as have been impressed into employment over and above the pre-war complement by the various well-known causes—loss of fortune, reduction of the standing army, increase in women's work, and so on. In other words, if the number of persons at present unemployed in Germany is deducted from the number of persons who normally are in employment, there remains still a greater percentage of the population actually in employment than before the War. (The figures taken —from the last census of employment, in 1925—for comparison with the pre-war figures given above are as follows: 32,000,000 employed persons, in a population of 62,000,000, or 51.3 per cent.)

Such reflections are poor comfort for any hungry man. They are, indeed, the very opposite of comforting; they only make German unemployment seem so much the more hopeless. The effects of the War drove millions into working for wages for their daily bread who in the past had had no need to do so; the illusory boom of the inflation period, the inflation of prices, the ubiquitous bureaucratization, and so on provided them with the opportunity of supporting themselves in industrial employment. The proletarianization of Germany produced by the War—the phenomenon is not in the slightest degree international; it is a German error to suppose it so—finds its clearest expression in this increase in the percentage of employed persons. If the crisis with its return to the "peace-time prices" is regarded as a sort of return to the normal peace standard, it is not so very surprising to find the additional employed persons recruited after the War now being dispensed with again. This gives the unemployment figure much more finality, and it becomes a duty to proceed to combat it by quite other means than through mere assistance of the unemployed, which carries with it the tacit assumption that the unemployment is transient, and that the unemployed only want "helping over" the "abnormal" period. If for a considerable section of those affected the unemployment is definitive, nothing but a return to the land can be of any help. Settlement on the land takes on then quite another significance, and is called for on quite another scale, from that of a mere device for relieving the municipal insurance funds.

From this point of view, however, the comparison between the German and the American economic system takes on quite a different aspect. It is quite true that the percentage of unemployment in the two countries is virtually the same; but that is altogether beside the question. If it is desired to compare the serviceability of two economic systems in the crisis, the thing that one must ask is not what percentage of the population each system turns into the street, but what percentage each system is able still to provide with work and food. The standard is not the last worker dismissed, but the last worker employed. From this point of view the picture offered by the statistics is completely changed. We see that, in spite of all the suffering and all the impoverishment, the German economic system is still able to give work to the same percentage of the population as before the War. America, on the contrary, is only able now to employ thirty-three to thirty-four per cent of her population in wage-earning occupations.

It does not follow that Germany is in any less trouble than the United States. On the contrary, the fact that so large a percentage in Germany entered after the War into employment for the first time is direct evidence of the poverty of the country. But the establishment of the actual situation is of importance to our diagnosis when we are searching for the real source of the malady. Unemployment first became strikingly noticeable in Germany, and the result was that unconsciously people got used to supposing that the malady had been incubated in Germany and had spread thence like some zymotic infection to the other, sounder economic systems. We begin now to understand why, when world trade began to shrink, unemployment was bound to become serious in Germany first: Germany had the greatest percentage of recently recruited additional wage-earners. We see, moreover, that, in spite of their incomparably better capital equipment, the other economic systems were not a bit healthier. On the contrary, considered in relation to unemployment, they were less healthy than Germany's—for the first duty of a national economic system is surely to feed its members. We begin to wonder whether the actual source of the infection is not, perhaps, to be found within the two Anglo-Saxon economic systems—for much the same is true of British conditions. Can it be, then, that the two richest national economic systems, the two that drew the largest gains from the War, are also the two sickliest? How could that be possible?

However, we do not want to inquire here into causes, but simply to ascertain the facts. But there is no getting rid of the fact just established, it emerges beyond possibility of contradiction, so soon as trade and industry are regarded from the point of view of the percentage of the population which remains in occupational employment. We think the Americans would do well to consider this fact. For, unlike the Frenchman, who will let you steal his world trade so long as he is sure of the *poule au pot* of Henri Quatre,[1] the Americans feel a responsibility and even ambition for world trade. They thought that they had discovered the philosophers' stone for humanity, the secret of perpetual prosperity; and now are their trade and industry to be suddenly the sickest of all?

THE FALL IN PRICES

While everybody knows only too well all about unemployment in Germany, one finds the layman in Germany, who is not himself a trader, usually hazy about the fall in prices. What does it matter, after all, to the layman if, according to Fisher, the American index number of wholesale prices (1926 prices being taken as 100) fell by the end of June 1931 to 70.3? What matters most to him is the German index number of consumable commodity prices, and that stood at the same date at 140.9 (1913 = 100). It is no help to him that in Germany the index number of the so-called *reagible Waren,* the goods that respond to world price movements—broken-up machinery, scrap iron, brass shavings, wool, hemp, flax, calfskin, and so on—has also fallen to 69.

We cannot refrain, however, for all that the fact of the fall in prices is common knowledge, from showing the extent of the fall, especially in relation to

[1] "I want every labourer in my kingdom to be able to put his chicken to boil on a Sunday." (Translator's note.)

pre-war prices, from a few instances. (See Table A, page 31.)

Why is it that, in spite of this, the cost of living is so much higher than before the War? Reply: the Table A contains only the prices of materials which are entirely or relatively little controlled by cartels or influenced by duties. A few more examples will show what the same set of figures looks like with controlled prices. (See Table B, page 31.)

Compare this with the movements of wheat in the world market. Wheat quotations (Northern III, f.o.b. Winnipeg, price in cents per 60 lbs.) were:

End of August 1929	146.25
End of November 1929	130.50
End of May 1930	107.69
End of August 1930	82.75
End of May 1931	51.00
End of June 1931	53.88

These few examples will have furnished us with some idea of the price movements, but the safest estimate will be got by returning to the index numbers. As recently as the end of July 1929, the American index number of wholesale prices, according to Fisher, who takes 1926 as 100, was still up to 99.2. At the end of June 1931 it was 70.3. The British wholesale-price index number (*Financial Times;* 1913 = 100) was 130.8 at the end of July 1929 and 90.5 at the end of June 1931. Thus the whole fall in prices is concentrated on the two years since July 1929; in these two years world market prices fell no less than

TABLE A

WHOLESALE PRICES OF A FEW IMPORTANT COMMODITIES

Goods and Market	*Kilo-grams*	*Annual average—prices in marks*[1]					*January 1931*	*July 3, 1931*	*Percentage of 1913*
		1913	*1927*	*1928*	*1929*	*1930*			
Copper (electrolytic), Berlin	100	146.19	126.58	140.54	173.85	127.43	97.43	85.50	58.5
Zinc, Hamburg	100	45.38	57.77	50.98	49.95	32.96	24.86	26.25	57.8
Raw cotton (American), Bremen	1	1.30	1.77	2.01	1.92	1.39	1.04	1.04	80.3
Artificial silk, Bremen	1	12.50	11.39	11.75	7.90	6.92	5.80	5.15	41.2
Wool, Buenos Aires	1	3.65	5.35	6.09	5.36	3.30	2.75	2.78	76.2
Coffee (Santos, sup.), Hamburg, less duty	50	66.50	84.49	108.06	98.36	60.40	46.22	49.00	73.7
Pork, Berlin	50	69.60	83.10	86.00	103.40	87.00	76.00	63.00	90.5
Rubber, Hamburg	1	6.19	3.46	2.05	1.93	1.11	0.77	0.61	9.9

TABLE B

Goods and Market	*Kilo-grams*	*Annual average—prices in marks*					*January 1931*	*July 3, 1931*	*Percentage of 1913*
		1913	*1927*	*1928*	*1929*	*1930*			
Wheat, Berlin	100	191.00	267.10	234.00	227.80	256.40	259.20	259.50	135.6
Rye, Berlin	100	155.50	249.00	239.10	192.40	161.90	156.30	211.00	135.6
Foundry pig iron, Oberhausen	100	74.50	83.33	82.00	83.89	83.91	78.00	78.00	104.7

[1] The German mark is approximately equivalent to an English shilling: 11.747 pence or 23.821 cents at par. —TRANSLATOR.

30 per cent. Never before in the history of the world has so rapid a decline occurred in so short a period.

This decline in prices, as is evident from the examples given, affects raw materials and agricultural produce alike. German agriculture has so far been protected from the effects of the decline by extraordinarily heavy protective duties, thanks to which the price of wheat in the German home market is two to two and a half times the world market price. It may be useful to quote a few more examples. For the sake of simplicity the actual fall in prices is given here at once:

FALL IN PRICES OF CERTAIN AGRICULTURAL PRODUCTS, IN PERCENTAGES

Product and Market	*Annual average*		*December 1930 compared with December 1929*
	1930 compared with 1929	*1930 compared with 1928*	
Wheat, Rotterdam	21	28	44
Rye, Rotterdam	43	53	54
Barley, Rotterdam	38	51	44
Oats, Buenos Aires	45	56	50
Maize, London	35	39	41
Rice, London	16	20	34
Fruit, Italy	35	47	42
Sugar, New York	28	42	39
Cocoa, London	22	39	35
Pepper, Hamburg	38	45	46
Soya beans, Hamburg	26	29	34
Flax, London	32	47	38
Jute, London	32	36	41
Butter, Copenhagen	19	22	27
Wool, London	38	51	36
Silk, London	29	28	46

It need scarcely be pointed out that these great falls in price mean a fall in the return from the yield of the harvests and accordingly a fall in the purchasing power of the agriculturists. The fall in the return from sales, and, accordingly, in the gross purchasing power, between 1929 and 1930 was estimated for Germany by the Institut für Konjunkturforschung at 11 per cent. And, with their high protective duties, the German agriculturists were in the most favoured situation. The Institute gives the following estimates of the fall in the gross purchasing power of the agriculturists for the year 1930 as compared with 1929:

10–15% in Germany, France, Great Britain, and Central America
15–20% in the United States and British India
20–25% in Italy, Czechoslovakia, and Brazil
25–30% in Australia, Japan, China, and Egypt
30–40% in Canada, Argentina, and Spain

What does all this mean in marks? Taking a general average, the reduction in the income of the agriculturists of the world in 1930 as compared with the preceding year may be estimated at some twenty-five to thirty milliards of gold marks. That is the fall in gross purchasing power. The fall in net purchasing power is less, since the prices of industrial products have also fallen, if less steeply, so that the farmer could buy more for a mark than the year before. Of this, more in a moment.

The distress implicit in these figures came suddenly on the farmers, while the barns were full and it was with difficulty that room was found in the granaries for the new crop alongside the stocks still in hand from the old one. For the old law that falling prices set goods moving seems no longer to be valid. What is the good of low prices if even at these the turnover grows less? So agriculture presents the spectacle which is characteristic of this crisis in every field of economic life—want through superfluity.

DECLINE IN PRODUCTION AND SHRINKAGE OF TRADE

We have already given above examples showing that the fall in prices has affected industrial raw materials equally with agricultural produce. The industrial finished product, however, has benefited only fractionally from this fall. We give here alongside one another the German index numbers for raw materials and finished products:

	End of June	
Index numbers for:	*1929*	*1931*
Industrial raw materials and semi-products	131.5	103.4
Industrial finished products	157.2	136.5

It will be seen that industrial raw materials and semi-products have experienced a decline in prices on a similar scale to agricultural produce, but finished products have fallen much less. This is partly the result of price agreements (though some of the principal industrial raw materials are also governed by cartels; iron, for instance); but there is also the circumstance that industry is not compelled to buy all the crops that God ordains to grow, while as soon as trade declines, it cuts down its own production. Thus, the parallel symptoms to the decline in agricultural prices have to be measured in industry not only in price figures but also in figures of production. And here the decline is plain for all to see. Once more we find the phenomenon of an international decline with strange regional variations. The German Konjunkturinstitut [1] estimates the decline in industrial production from the last peak of good trade (a date varying somewhat for the different countries) to the end of April 1931 as follows:

	Percentage of decline
Germany	32
Poland	32
Canada	30
United States	29
Great Britain	26
Finland	23
Sweden	21
France	9

This decline in industrial production will find direct expression in the valuation of the shares quoted in the international stock exchanges. If one takes the average price of the principal shares in each of the various centres at the end of December 1927 as 100, one gets the following figures of price movements in the early months of last year:

[1] I. e., Institut für Konjunkturforschung.—TRANSLATOR.

Stock Exchange	End of 1927 = 100 December 27, 1930	February 28, 1931	May 30, 1931
Berlin	46.9	49.7	42.0
London	50.0	47.9	36.1
Paris	92.1	96.7	76.4
Brussels	55.8	63.0	39.7
Amsterdam	50.6	57.6	43.6
Basel-Zurich	67.4	76.7	65.6
Milan	75.5	84.5	71.8
New York	76.8	94.9	71.9

Decline in agricultural purchasing power and decline in industrial production combine to give the picture of a general shrinkage of trade. This shrinkage finds plain expression in the figures of foreign trade turnover. The aggregate turnover in the foreign trade of forty-eight countries taken together amounted in 1930 to 204.5 milliards of gold marks, against 253.2 milliards in 1929. The decline continued in 1931: the aggregate turnover of these countries for the first quarter of 1931 was 39.8 milliards of gold marks, against 64.4 milliards in the first quarter of 1929 and 56.8 in 1930.

Nor is any sign yet discernible of the ending of this process of shrinkage. On the contrary, every attempt to discover grounds of renewed hope has so far been replied to only by a severer set-back. The table of stock-exchange quotations just given shows very plainly how in every centre at the beginning of the year the bourse tried in vain to awaken hope, and also how the proverbial optimism of the Americans ventured furthest in this direction—in vain.

Not since it has been possible to speak of an interdependent world economy of the capitalist type has any crisis so apparently unending been known. The most sensitive indicator is the movement of security prices. In the great crisis of 1900 prices began to climb up again after 29 months, in the crisis of 1906 after 26 months. The present downward movement has now continued in Germany for 52 months.

THE MONEY MARKET

The money market shows the corresponding picture: on the one hand, the price of money extraordinarily depressed (in June 1931 private discount rates fell in London to 2.10 per cent, in Zurich to 1.13, and in Amsterdam actually to 0.93 per cent); on the other hand, scarcely any money to be had the moment it becomes a question of long-term loans, and a slump in share issues. Never before was the difference between the interest rates for short-term and for long-term money so great. Once more, want cheek by jowl with superfluity. The amount of money seeking investment was shown by the issue of the 3⅛ per cent American loan, offered to the public last June. The loan, amounting to eight hundred million dollars, was subscribed seven and a half times over.

Up to now the classic theory had been that cheap money encourages enterprise; that, accordingly, a crisis would have reached its natural termination when discount rates had sunk low enough. Are they to sink yet lower? Every rule for the mechanism of economic life seems this time to have been abrogated.

In the latter part of last year the note banks of some countries suddenly made rapid increases in their discount rates. Needless to say, this increase was not to be interpreted as it would be in normal times. For it was decided on, not as a brake on excessive private enterprise, but to protect the gold standard in these countries; not because too much credit was being asked for for fresh enterprises, but because a very strong inclination was being evidenced to turn credit into gold. Ultimately these countries were forced off the gold standard.

It was not our purpose to give a complete enumeration of the phenomena of the crisis. All that we aimed at was to recall briefly what there is about this crisis that is peculiar to it, and in what respects it differs from other crises. The special features of this crisis we have found to be: it is of extraordinary severity and extraordinarily prolonged; it is an international crisis with curious regional variations; it is a general crisis, not attacking merely a section of the economic system after the fashion of, say, an industrial crisis or any other partial crisis, but affecting every part of the economic system, and producing a universal shrinkage of the whole of the world's economic activities; it is characterized by the paradoxical juxtaposition of want and superfluity: want among the farmers, with superfluity in the overfilled granaries; want of orders in industry with a superfluity never before known in productive capacity; want of long-term credits with a superfluity of day-to-day money.

How can it be possible to find, for these heterogeneous and almost mutually contradictory symptoms, a common explanation?

Chapter Three

THE FIRST QUESTION: THE CRISIS

The question of the causes of the crisis has been put and answered in so many quarters that we can easily arrive at the answer: we shall simply examine the answers that have been given and adopt those that we find correct. Why go to the trouble of thinking out for oneself what has been thought out already on all sides?

We will apply, however, to the master smith and not the journeyman. In turning to the International Chamber of Commerce, that august assemblage of the élite of the business world, we need have no fear of being led astray by the idiosyncrasies of an individual thinker, perhaps a crank.

The Council of the International Chamber of Commerce adopted at its session of December 5, 1930 a resolution in which it gave the causes of the crisis as follows:

1. A general increase in productive capacity that has temporarily outstripped the rate of increase in population and in the capacity of consumption.

2. Following upon a long period of decline in world commodity prices, a farther sharp and excessive fall in prices, especially in raw materials and foodstuffs, not only too rapid but also too extensive to enable costs of production to be adapted, and throwing retail prices out of equilibrium to wholesale prices. Immediate recovery from the prevailing price depression is delayed by the postponement of liquidation in stocks (inventories).

3. The world-spread agricultural crisis.

4. The unprecedented extent of industrial unemployment.

5. The prolonged malaise caused by political unrest.

6. The partial or complete closing of some of the world's most important markets.

7. The slow readjustment of national to international economic situations by reason of the varied bases chosen for monetary stabilization.

8. Barriers to enterprise and investment imposed in many places by an unusual disparity between long term and short term money rates.

9. The heavy fall in the price of silver that has further reduced the purchasing power of one-third of the world's population.

10. The forcing on the world markets of large quantities of grain, raw materials, and semi-finished products by Soviet Russia at prices less than the normal cost of production.

11. The levying in many countries of taxation, to meet unprecedented national and international indebtedness.

12. Excessive incursions of the State into the domain of private enterprise, which are clearly hindering and in some cases actually preventing the necessary accumulation of private capital and the inducements to private enterprise and venture.

We do not know whether the cloud overhanging the number 12 led the Chamber of Commerce to close its list there. When the retiring president of the Chamber, Georges Theunis, read the list at the Washington Congress, he at once added a thirteenth cause: "Commercial policy and the Customs tariffs maintained in most countries of the world." The next moment, however, a fourteenth presented itself: "Excessive mechanization by means of borrowed capital."

This list could, indeed, be further extended without difficulty. For one thing, the factors enumerated are far from all having the rank of causes; causes and symptoms are arbitrarily mixed up. We have made the acquaintance in the preceding chapter of a whole series of the factors adduced (2, 3, 4, 8)—as symptoms. And Point 12 is a whole program.

It is certainly surprising that the Chamber of Commerce should not have taken the trouble to separate causes and symptoms. For this list is not an arbitrary, chance production like so many resolutions; it was regarded as exact enough to be made the basis of a questionnaire which was dispatched to the various national groups, so that they might be guided by this list in reporting to the Washington Congress on the trade and industry of their own country. Moreover, among the true causes that remain in the questionnaire, there are mixed up indiscriminately general causes, affecting the whole course of economic life, and regional causes applicable only to a part of the earth's surface.

We will try to bring a little order into this chaos of causes. To that end we will go through the various components of the economic process itself, and search for the possible root cause of the trouble.

PRODUCTION

The Chamber of Commerce puts in the first place among the causes of the crisis the general increase in productive capacity. That is only too familiar a phenomenon in the crises of the nineteenth century: over-production, beyond a certain limit, leading to falling prices, restriction of production, and the other symptoms of crisis. Such crises had the practical function of inducing a pause in production through which the normal relation between consumption and production could be restored. Have we not related how in the present crisis the granaries are filled to overflowing, the stocks piling up? What is more natural than to explain the present crisis on the analogy of its predecessors and to attribute it once more to overproduction? The latest increase in production, occasioned by the rationalization carried out in recent years, is plain for all to see. It has often enough been explained how, in consequence of the new methods, a miner can now extract as much as three or four could before, how motors are assembled on a moving platform, how agriculture has multiplied its crops through chemical manuring and tractors and has in addition the use of the acreage that its beasts of burden used to eat up, how a bank-clerk can enter up a whole army of accounts simultaneously with the booking-machine. Thus this crisis might seem to be just one more crisis of over-production, and one might take the whole riddle as solved.

This view is very widely held. Over-production is the first explanation that one is constantly offered. And no one is likely to dream of questioning the facts of the increased production. But does this explanation bring us to the root of the matter?

So long as the capitalist theory of economics has been taught, increase of production has always been accounted the bringer of all progress, the strengthener of trade and industry; and now is it suddenly to be the scapegoat for all our troubles? How long ago is it that, especially in Germany, one read in every newspaper that only increase of production could save us, that that alone could enable us to preserve ourselves from ruin; and are we now to turn round and charge it with having brought down on us the curse of the crisis? It is precisely the people, too, who are now talking the loudest about "crisis of rationalization" and "ill-judged capital expenditure" that were the most eloquent preachers of rationalization five years ago. What were our captains of industry really thinking of when they went in for rationalization—mostly with dearly borrowed money? Did they actually give no thought to the question who was going to take from them their increase of output? We shall hesitate as yet to believe that they can have made their calculations so badly.

The next question in the matter of over-production is: Where exactly is this over-production? In agriculture, or in industry, or in mining, or in transport? Obviously in the whole lot of them at once. We have heard often enough that the decline in prices is general. So far as rationalization is concerned, there has been just as much rationalization in agriculture (not, indeed, in Germany) as in mining and in industry. The over-production is general—it is not by any inadvertence that the International Chamber of Commerce speaks of the *general* increase in productive capacity. As we saw, the crisis is not a partial crisis, not, for instance, merely an industrial or merely an agrarian crisis, but a universal one.

Now, it is not a piece of wisdom in the private possession of the writer, but one of the few facts with regard to which the exponents of political economy are in agreement, that there is no such thing as *general* over-production. "Over"-production is a relative matter; the measure of it is the capacity of the rest of trade and industry to produce and buy. If everyone produces more, everyone has more to offer and everyone can also buy more. Then the fall in prices is made good by increased turnover. The consequences of "general" over-production are thus a general reduction of prices accompanied by an increase in consumption, a general increase in the standard of living, never in the life of man a general crisis.

Let it not be objected that all this is mere theory. We may make our meaning clear in this way: Suppose that there were to come back today, or, better, were to have come back in 1913, a man who had lived a century or a century and a half before. The first thing that would have struck him would have been the masses of shops occupying the ground floors of our town buildings—for in his day the citizens still lived on the ground floor. And he would ask, in astonishment, where ever had all the enormous accumulations of stored-up goods come from—had we all become Crœsuses? In comparison with his day we should all be utterly swamped, floundering in "general overproduction." The general level of consumption has risen in comparison with his time in a degree that none of his contemporaries could have foreseen—but that had nothing whatever to do with any crisis. Until now, the increase in the level of consumption has been the unquestioned criterion of economic progress—why should it suddenly cease to be so? It is impossible, moreover, to suppose that consumption has reached its topmost limit and is no longer capable of increase.

On both sides, in agriculture and in industry, we have an increase in goods produced and in productive capacity. But why cannot the surpluses on the two sides be exchanged, why cannot the excess production be taken up by an excess consumption? *Where is the barrier?* That is the problem. The "general overproduction" is no problem.

Some readers will object: "How wrong-headed all this argumentation is can best be seen from conditions in Germany. German agriculture has not been able to increase its productive capacity in the same measure as German industry, which rationalized for the purpose of increasing its exports. There can never be any question of German agriculture gaining through increased production sufficient purchasing power to enable it to take up the excess production of German industry." That objection is quite sound for German conditions. But if it were applicable also to world trade and industry, it would have led one to expect a special agrarian crisis in Germany (which does in fact exist), while in the rest of the world the simultaneous increases in agricultural and industrial production would have produced falling prices, a general increase in turnover, and a raising of the standard of living. That is just what the various industrial and agricultural capitalists did expect when they rationalized: they all calculated on increased turnover, they all felt themselves to be little Fords. Why did it not turn out as expected?

And, finally, if it were true that we had a crisis of over-production, what would be the logical way to combat it? Are we to stop the moving platforms, scrap the expensive machines, let the tractors rust and bring out the horses again? For, be it carefully noted, it is not merely production that has been increased, not merely, say, the gift vouchsafed of a record harvest, but the *capacity* for production. It would be of no avail to lay idle fifty per cent of the productive capacity: so soon as it was in use once more, we should have the same crisis back again! If the general capacity for over-production—as, to be more precise, one ought to put it—were really to blame, we should be in an endemic crisis of eternal duration. Then there would be no other way out than to make half the means of production *kaput*—to scrap them.

But all this logic is an old story. On these same grounds in the past the hand-loom weavers declared that there were too many power-looms. To talk of a crisis called forth by rationalization is the logic of the machine-wreckers.

CONSUMPTION

All these considerations are no private discovery of the writer's. The political economists have long recognized that the talk of over-production will not hold water. Accordingly, the search for causes began to be transferred to the other end—to consumption. And now the old quidnuncs' problem of the hen and the egg turned up in a new guise—what came first, over-production or "underconsumption"? Once more, too, talk of the "buyers' strike" became audible.

Ideas of that sort are excusable at best in an early stage of the crisis. Today if anyone wants to tell us that our "underconsumption" is a contributory cause of the general crisis, the best thing we can all do is politely to change the subject. It is only possible to talk with reason of a "buyers' strike" as a voluntary restriction of consumption, at a particular psychological moment of a downward movement of prices, when the consumer has become doubtful of the course of prices and temporarily postpones buying in anticipation of a further fall.

All that is characteristic only of general uncertainty. "Underconsumption" in the sense of restriction of consumption is actually a symptom of the crisis. There is no more prospect of successfully attacking the problem of the crisis from this side than from that of production.

GOLD

Since the fall in prices is general and has affected all goods equally—so far as supply has not been influenced by restrictions of production, or prices themselves by duties and price agreements—the pundits arrived long ago at the idea that the cause of the fall in prices should, perhaps, not be sought on the side of the goods at all, not in supply or demand, but on the side of the payment medium, and so, in the last resort, of gold. It is, indeed, not quite easy to imagine how *all* goods could suddenly be produced in increased quantity and offered in a rush. On the other hand, there is a brilliant simplicity about the solution that the measure, the gold, has become scarcer and that that is why prices have fallen. The matter is made yet more exciting by the circumstance that, years ago, when all the world was still confident that prosperity was going to last for ever and prices slowly but surely to go on going up, an economist, Gustav Cassel, predicted a fall in prices owing to the growing scarcity of gold. Then, in a night, for no definite reason that could be discovered, came the general crisis, and, at a loss for an explanation, people seized on the one already offered, and the scientists seemed to have put their finger on the spot.

It very soon proved, however, that the explanation did not fit. Cassel himself states that the quantity of gold must increase 2.8 per cent per annum if prices are to remain constant. In recent years the gold production has not reached this level, but has remained rather below it. But the inadequate fresh supplies of gold could only result in drops in prices of at most the same order of magnitude. There can be no explanation here for the fall in prices since 1929 of about ten times as much.

It is not suggested that the phenomenon to which Cassel drew attention has no existence. In coming decades it may attain a reality of which we have as yet no conception. Last year's *Year Book of the Union of South Africa* (the principal gold-producing country) published the results of an inquiry in which it is predicted, on statistical evidence shown, that there will be a steady fall in the production of gold in coming years. The following estimate of gold production is given, in pounds sterling:

1931	42,600,000	1936	34,400,000
1932	43,700,000	1940	25,500,000
1933	42,400,000	1945	15,500,000
1934	40,700,000	1946	11,700,000
1935	39,030,000	1947	10,000,000

Let us leave the future to fight its own battles. Sufficient for today that in the next two years gold production is still to remain relatively constant.

It is plain, then, that the gold theory in this form, which lays the blame for the crisis on the inadequacy of the quantity of gold in the world, is only a matter for the future to concern itself with. Nevertheless, the view that the present crisis is attributable to shortage of gold has a large number of adherents and is continually being given fresh expression. Its advocates honestly believe that it would help the world if tomorrow, somewhere in Africa or California, there were suddenly discovered a gigantic outcrop of gold. Comparatively recently Herr Tyska, of Hamburg, expressed in the *Deutscher Ökonomist* the view that "the fall in prices which we are experiencing at present is due, or at all events mainly due, to the reduction in the output of gold, and thus arises from the increase in the value of gold and therefore of money." The only evidence he offers is the fact that gold production reached its peak in 1915. No figures or proportions are given; on the contrary, the writer in the *Deutscher Ökonomist* alleges that "only the most recent years show an increase, and that only a very moderate one." That purports to be scientific demonstration.

Since the gold theory in this quantitative form, in which account is taken only of the quantity of gold available, is untenable, critics in Germany were inclined to reject in advance the quite different theory of gold put forward by Sir Henry Strakosch in his important article in the *Economist* of July 5, 1930; although Strakosch advances something altogether different.

Strakosch also thinks quantitatively, writes of the quantity of gold. But by that he does not mean the absolute amount of the gold available in the world's economic system; nor does he refer to the scarcity resulting from declining gold production. He refers only to the quantity of gold actually in use as the basis of credit, and its diminution, or, more precisely, its failure to be put to use, as a result of unequal distribution. He writes much less of a problem of quantity than of one of distribution. Gold stocks which are withdrawn from monetary employment through accumulation in the note banks, and so lose their function as regulators of trade and industry, are "sterilized." For gold on which no credit is built up is no longer performing any monetary function.

When Strakosch wrote his article, he was arguing on the basis of the gold stocks in the hands of the note banks at the end of 1929. He gives the amount of gold in the hands of the Bank of France as 336,000,000 pounds; that in the hands of the American Federal Reserve Bank as 802,000,000 pounds; and the gold held in Britain and Germany as only 146,000,000 and 112,000,000 pounds. This accumulation of gold in particular centres has, in Strakosch's view, produced a *relative* reduction of purchasing power. From this there has resulted a slowing down of the process of exchange and of consumption, whence have come finally the slump in prices and the general depression. The world, he argues, is robbing itself of the advantages of increasing production and the creation of wealth if it does not take care "in co-operation" that the monetary employment of gold is assured. From this we get as the true reason of the fall in prices and the world depression "the deflationary effect of the sterilization of gold."

Since Strakosch published his article, we have grown a year older. Let us see whether in the period during which the crisis has continued we can actually observe the gold movement which he singled out for criticism, and whether it continued further during last year. The monetary stocks of gold in the world were as follows, in millions of gold marks:

	End 1928	*Mid 1931*	*Change*
United States ...	17,386	20,633	plus 3,247
France	5,260	9,280	" 4,020
Great Britain	3,352	3,528	" 176
Switzerland	593	841	" 248
Holland	807	913	" 106
Sweden	266	269	" 3
Above six countries together .	27,664	35,465	Increase 7,801
Rest of the world	19,552	15,923	Decrease 3,629

Thus, simultaneously with the further accentuation of the crisis, there has been an unmistakable further increase in the inequality of the distribution of gold. *This parallel development of one-sided accumulation of gold and growing acuteness of the crisis was not to be expected under any other theory of the crisis;* indeed, other theories, such, for instance, as the over-production theory, took no account whatever of the possibility that the distribution of gold might have something to do with the question. Thus, there seems every reason to suppose that Strakosch is right in finding a connexion between the distribution of gold and the crisis—though we will leave open for the present the question whether the connexion is one of cause and effect. In spite of this, Strakosch's theory has been rejected by most of the German scientists. The principal line of argument against it has been that in recent years, in spite of every inequality in the distribution of gold, the general volume of credit has grown much more rapidly than the gold reserves (Herrmann in the *Magazin der Wirtschaft,* July 25, 1930; Palyi in the *Berliner Tageblatt,* July 27, 1930). The semi-official German Konjunkturinstitut devoted one of its weekly reports (No. 36, December 3, 1930) to the gold theory. It considered itself to be in a position to demonstrate that "the quantity of credit possible on the basis of a given stock of gold is by no means so narrowly restricted as the adherents of the gold thesis assume." The report closes with the statement that "the provision of gold can scarcely be in itself the deciding cause of the change in the economic situation." "If the quantity of credit in world trade is but little influenced by the supply of gold, the customary assumption of a causal association between gold and prices can no longer be upheld. One must assume for the long-wave movements in trade and industry . . . some cause as yet not definitely identified."

Must trade and industry wait patiently until the experts have tracked down this "cause as yet not definitely identified"? Meanwhile the experiences of recent months have demonstrated in the most astonishing fashion the hard and fast restrictions imposed on the "quantity of credit possible on the basis of a given stock of gold."

In contrast to this attitude of the German experts, the views of Strakosch have been generally accepted in the Anglo-Saxon countries. When gold conferences are demanded, when Mr. Winston Churchill exclaims in the House of Commons that there is no sense in digging gold up out of a hole in the earth in order to bury it in another hole in the vaults of the Bank of France—all that is the purest Strakoschism. Nay, more—the whole course of the British abandonment of the gold standard, hard as the decision may have been for the country to take, aimed as it was against France, is to be regarded as in the last resort the outcome of Strakosch's views.

But it has also been the constant theme of the German newspapers, for months past, that France's hoarding of gold is withdrawing gold from trade, or reducing the quantity of the notes based on gold available for world trade, and so reducing the world's purchasing power. Is not this spread of the Strakosch line of argument a proof of its force, with all the German experts against it?

Let us see how the gold movement summarized in the last table stands with reference to the needs of note cover. Of the gold reserves shown, the following amounts were not required as note cover (in millions of gold marks):

	End 1929	*Mid 1930*
United States	7,634	10,460
France	1,780	3,508
Great Britain	435	1,348
Switzerland	94	185
Holland	442	505
Sweden	25	75
Total	10,410	16,081

That is the quantity of gold which, in Strakosch's phrase, is "sterilized." The quantity of bank-notes which could be based on this gold amounts, according to the bank laws of the various countries, to two and a half to three times as much. We estimated above the reduction in the return which the agriculturists of the world were able to secure in 1930, in spite of good harvests, at twenty-five to thirty milliards of gold marks.

In the presence of agreements so close, what is the sense of waiting, as the German experts propose, for the establishment of some other "cause as yet not definitely identified"? But, above all, Strakosch's language is the language of the Anglo-Saxon victor States. The Anglo-Saxon does his economic thinking instinctively in terms of gold. The German, with his preference for abstractions, prefers to think in terms of credit; he prides himself on his knowledge that the movement of credit is in a certain degree independent of that of gold—until the unhappy day comes when he has to admit that this relative independence of credit from gold no longer exists if the credit-giver thinks it does not. The whole crisis in payment media in Germany last year was based psychologically on the fact that credit, even short-term credit, was regarded as an independent thing, a thing with which, for instance, factories were built—and among the experts the Strakosch theory is rejected in the same spirit. It is once more the same mistake that was made in 1914 when it was argued that no world war could possibly break out because the world's credit network had grown much too complicated.

But, however that may be, the gold language that is talked in the victor countries, especially the Anglo-Saxon countries, is in any case the ruling language, and it offers us Germans our only opportunity of coming to terms with the victors. We are the vanquished, we have every reason to learn the victors' language. There may be something touching in the absolute incapacity of the German scientist for any sort of Machiavellism; but, after all, all political economy is a practical science; after all, the main thing is that something has got to be done, and that is of more importance than to enjoy the superiority of maintaining that the view with which the other party is credited is erroneous, while one goes on with one's speculations concerning the "cause as yet not definitely identified."

Are we actually suggesting to Science that she should accept as true, simply on practical grounds, a theory that she has found to be false? We hear the swelling chorus of anathema of her outraged priests. But what is it exactly that is maintained in the Strakosch theory? It gives as the cause of the crisis the deflationary effect of the sterilization of gold by the note banks. But the flow of gold to the note banks is, after all, not the primary variable. Why does gold flow away from some of the note banks and towards others? It really is not because the receiving banks are drawing in the gold out of malice and uncharitableness. Their mere decision to have it would never bring it. We ought readily to believe the statement of Monsieur Morel, the president of the Bank of France, at last year's general meeting that the bank "has not moved a finger to obtain the money from other countries." And America was protesting at one time against the undesired stream of incoming gold, fearing that it would bring increased prices within the country. The flow of gold is produced precisely in the same way as the flow of water or of electricity, through a fall of potential, and continues until equilibrium is restored. But what produces the fall of potential which has set gold flowing into the note banks of France and of the United States? These countries' credit balances of international payments. Sir Henry Strakosch is silent as to that.

But if the stream of gold did not flow at the bidding of the note banks concerned, perhaps it is their doing that it did not flow away again? What might the note banks have done to set all this stagnant gold flowing off once more and to make the distribution of gold in the world more equal?—Either they would have had to make a really enormous reduction in their discount rates, and accordingly to bring more notes into circulation in their country, to increase the internal purchasing power, at the certain risk of increasing prices (France objected to that and preferred the path of sterilization); or else they would have had to export capital and lend money abroad—as America did, with the same energy with which France refrained.

That is all there is in the conception of "sterilization." It does not look back and ask how the unequal distribution of gold occurred; it looks forward and demands that the maldistribution shall be got rid of. It is not a conception of a fact, but of a rule; at its basis there lies the regulative requirement that the world's gold stocks should be so administered as to fulfil their monetary function; that is, that they should be made full use of for the building up of credit. That is all that the theory says; it refrains from pronouncing on causes. The whole Strakosch theory is pragmatic, like Anglo-Saxon thought; hence its failure to be understood in Germany. None of the German critics recognized its regulatory emphasis; they were in search of its statement of causes, and, finding none, they rejected the whole theory in favour of a "cause as yet not definitely identified." As a pronouncement upon causes, however, the Strakosch theory stands beyond true and false, for it refrains from any pronouncement on causes.

But how can the writer maintain that? Did he not himself state just now that Strakosch described the cause as the "deflationary effect of the sterilization of gold"?

Here the regulatory conception of sterilization is given as cause. Obviously: the crisis is continuing, the unequal distribution of gold is not being remedied, and *therefore* the cause of the crisis is that that is not being done which ought to be done (the true pragmatic touch!); that is, the gold is not being put to monetary use. How the unequal distribution of gold *originally* came about is not asked because Strakosch is not concerned with that.

But, apart from that, the whole talk about gold is only a clothing of the issue, a play with metaphor, a discussion from the angle of the measure. The layman has the instinctive feeling that there is something unnatural in thinking from gold as a starting-point, a sort of inversion of the natural order of things. When one says that the movement of goods on the market and their price are determined by gold, is it not something like saying that the electromotor is operated by the voltameter? In actual fact the electromotor is operated through the fall in the electric potential, which no man has yet seen, and economic values move in accordance with falls in the economic potentials, which also no man has yet seen, but which stand in the books as debtor and creditor and are measured in gold. The measure matters relatively little; any other would do, provided only that it is recognized by all those who are affected by the fall in the economic potential—and it will not be so easy to find a better measure than gold. But it is important not to imagine, as our apostles of inflation do, that if one throws away the gold measure, one gets rid at the same time of the fall in potential which was measured in gold. All that one can do by altering the measure is to substitute a new dummy fall for the existing one; and even that only for a time, until the dummy is seen through; the actual fall in potential is there all the time.

Those who imagine that the world level of prices could be raised and the whole crisis got rid of if the *quantity* of gold were increased (the adherents of the quantitative theory of the crisis) are like a doctor who might propose to get rid of his patient's fever by changing the quantity of mercury in his clinical thermometer. There is no denying that the thermometer could be brought in that way back to normal; but not the patient. It is quite easy to form a picture of what would happen with gold if, say, there were discovered tomorrow a great new gold-field: the fate of the existing gold is a plain enough guide. This quantitative theory mixes up cause and measure; we must reject it. Strakosch does not let himself be caught by any such fallacy. He makes no mention anywhere of the quantity of gold, only of its distribution; and not from the point of view of its origin, but from that of the way to get rid of it, or the way it is being maintained. His theory could be formulated without ever mentioning gold. It would run then as follows: In world trade there are differences in value levels between the various nations, and these are not being brought to equilibrium in the way demanded by the classical theory of banking. These differences of value level draw away purchasing power from some of the nations, while in the remaining, more favoured nations no corresponding new purchasing power is created. The result is that world trade as a whole becomes impoverished and prices have to give way.—There we have the contents of Strakosch's theory without its cloth of gold.

There is no reason why such a theory should be rejected. Sir Henry Strakosch was the first to point out an anomaly in world trade—that of the unequal distribution of gold. He did not state the cause of the anomaly, but he showed what happens if this disturbing element is not removed. He did so in a way that compelled the world to listen. His line of thought became the world's.

His theory springs from the way of thinking of a financier who believes in leaving trade to adjust itself. He established the fact of a diseased condition, he did not assign a cause to it, but he knew the therapy that would remove it; and now he sees with horror that this therapy is not being applied, but its opposite —"sterilization." But while we accept his diagnosis, it only adds to our despair. Is there the slightest prospect that the note banks of the victor States will throw out again the gold that they have garnered in their vaults? France has made plain enough how little inclined she is to lend money abroad.

Not only, however, is nothing being done to remedy the unequal distribution of gold, but the inequality is growing from day to day. Again and again one reads of new consignments of gold, and usually France is the consignee. But under present conditions every such consignment means that many times its value, in the form of the purchasing power that could be built up on it, is actually lost to world trade; the world turnover grows so much the more meagre. Plainly, the primary cause, which first produced the unequal distribution and so threw the world's trade out of equilibrium, continues in full operation. For us that means that we must bestir ourselves to discover it.

Thus, the gold theory in its turn has failed to bring us to the root cause of the crisis. The quantitative theory proved to be an unmistakable mare's-nest. The very different theory of Sir Henry Strakosch, on the other hand, proved to be by no means as mistaken as the German experts represented it. It established, to begin with, the existence of a symptom of crisis of the utmost importance and brought to our notice once more the whole menace of the situation, since nothing is being done to remove this symptom—on the contrary, it is assuming more serious dimensions every day. It spoke, furthermore, the gold language that the Germans should have every reason themselves to adopt, for everyone must master it who wants to come to terms with the world. And, on top of all this, it provided us with a guiding idea which may serve us further in the pursuit of the cause.

Of the cause itself, it is quite true, we remain as ignorant as ever.

PRICE FORMATION

There are others who share the view that the cause of the evil lies not with the goods, but with the prices. Not with the gold that is the measure of value, however, but with the actual price formation. The price that should indicate value has not, they think, been allowed free play, but has been falsified by subjecting it to artificial influences. The cartels have held up prices and held back stocks. The result has been that the world market has not been allowed to adjust itself step by step to a new price level resulting from the increased production. Now we are all in trouble; the artificially fixed prices are in some cases so remote from the world market level that we are in despair of ever getting them back to it. Meanwhile stocks are piling up, turnover is dwindling, purchasing power is dwindling with it, and the evil once set going is growing automatically, for every remedy attempted comes back to fresh price restrictions, which take us further and further from the objective of a free world market price.

How thoroughly perplexed people are in regard to

the question of price formation and price restriction may be illustrated from the fact that almost at every sentence one can bring along an objector who maintains its exact opposite. If there are some who say that the elimination of the free market has upset the equilibrium of world trade, that there is nothing for it but to restore the conditions of the free market, that the free play of forces and the unrestricted world market price would cure us all—there are others who declare that that would be the ruin of us all, that the only thing that has so far kept chaos at arm's length is price restriction, and that only a "sane cartel policy" can save the market and keep trade going.

We cannot undertake to pursue this controversy, argument by argument. We are only inquiring into the cause of the universal crisis. The facts brought forward one by one are accurate in themselves; the only question is what effect they have. It is true that when, in 1928, there came the giant's march of the record harvest, the wheat stocks were held up, in order not to let prices sag at once, just as, in the past, stocks of coffee, sugar, cocoa, cotton, rubber had been "valorized." But how long did the defence of prices last? The price of wheat slumped to a record low level, sugar fell to one third of pre-war, the collapse of coffee prices was such that in Brazil the guns went off: the whole set of valorizations did nothing—in those markets—but delay the catastrophe for two years. It was a speculation on harvest failures, a speculation like any other, and a very costly one for the "big capitalists" concerned—much Government money went with it—the "big capitalists" who are accounted the cause of all the evil. In all this there is no answer to be found for our inquiry. If speculation aims at getting over the difficulty of an unexpectedly large inrush of goods by discounting the chances of a less lavish future, there is nothing much in that. Two new questions, indeed, arise: How did the valorizations become possible and necessary? As to the necessity, whence came this sudden incursion of goods, and how was it that there were further ones of equal dimensions in the years that followed? Here we have once more the question of increase of production and rationalization. As to the possibility, whence came the money for the valorization? For if there had been none available, the harvest would have had to be disposed of, as it had to be later, when the crash came.

The valorization policy of the cartels only resulted in making the crisis more abrupt, more of a crash when it came. It is to that policy that it is mainly due that the outbreak of the crisis is associated in the public mind with the crash on the New York Stock Exchange, as though that were the cause of the whole crisis. In reality the cartels' policy of valorization was nothing more than an attempt to ward off the crisis which was already on the march. The fact that the attempt was made shows, at the same time, that the economic leaders had not the faintest idea two years ago of the amount of reconstruction that trade and industry were going to have to face.

Other cartel prices are still holding their own: iron above all, coal, potash, nickel, aluminium. They are doing their work: prices are considerably above pre-war. But these products are not world trade and not life. One can gauge from them how far the effectiveness of cartels and syndicates extends. Considerable as their range of influence is, it is not identical with the crisis—the only thing that matters to our purpose. Their activities are an attempt to ward off the crisis, and presuppose the coming of the crisis.

TARIFFS

The same is obviously true of the customs duties. Duties are, of course, equally with export bounties, nothing else than means of influencing prices, though in this case it is the State that operates them. Accordingly, thanks to the authority of the State, they promptly have their effect. It is the State's doing that the cost of living in Germany today is substantially higher than, for instance, in Germany's neighbour country Czechoslovakia—that "wage paradise" of many admiring observers—if, for another instance, in Germany, the land of the beet, sugar costs double the pre-war price, while it has sunk on the world market to one third of pre-war. Viewed, however, from the angle of the crisis, all these are defensive measures, desperate attempts to protect particular groups of occupied persons, to save their purchasing power for the "home market."

Certainly all protective duties—and almost every

week brings new ones—are just so many hindrances to the fluidity of the market, are means of laying low a proportion of the turnover, and stages on the road to further shrinkage of trade. They originate, however, as defensive measures, aimed at warding off an existing evil; they are reactions. Enormously as they influence the world's trade turnover, they owe their existence to the law of action and reaction. To see in them the cause of the crisis is to mix up cause and counteraction.

Even supposing the cause of the crisis were to lie in the duties, what then? The tragedy of the German-Austrian Customs Union has shown how impossible it is to remove even a single customs barrier. If we must defer our hopes of any improvement until the Governments have decided in unison to pull down the customs barriers, we may as well bury our hopes at once.

In customs duties we have inspected the last remaining field of the economic mechanism—distribution. For tariff barriers are the essential obstacle to distribution in the world market; the actual apparatus of distribution is in excellent condition. Hindrances to distribution in home trade—the gulf, for instance, between wholesale and retail prices—may bring up the index number of the cost of living as compared with the index number of wholesale trade, but may be left out of account in an inquiry into world trade.

Production, consumption, payment medium, prices, distribution—what remains for us to consider?

Credit? The International Chamber of Commerce mentions in its list of causes the difference between the interest rates for short-term and long-term credits. We have already seen that this is a symptom of the crisis, not the cause.

Alas! We must surely abandon any idea of discovering the cause in the actual mechanism of the market. This crisis is not a crisis like the others of the nineteenth century, it is not to be explained through the laws of the market. Somewhere there must be a barrier that is preventing surplus and want from equating. But we have not yet succeeded in finding it.

Since the cause is not to be discovered in the market, other observers have long been declaring that they have found it in special, geographical causes, operating from one quarter of the world to bring the whole world into disorder.

REGIONAL CAUSES

The first to be mentioned is the loss of the Russian and Chinese markets and lately of much of the Indian market. The inquiry of the League of Nations Commission, recently published, starts from this as the cardinal cause. (*Course and Phases of the World Economic Depression;* Geneva, 1931. Cf. also the Report of the Commission d'Étude pour l'Union Européenne on the economic depression, League of Nations printed paper No. C 284, M 134.)

It goes without saying that the loss of markets of such importance must have its effect on world trade, and it would be absurd to contest the fact. Only—the Russian market has been lost since 1918; and the fact that conditions in China are making a resumption of trade on the old scale impossible for a long time to come has been patent since about 1925. Meanwhile capitalist enterprise in trade and industry, the main virtue of which is its ready adaptability, should surely have been able to adjust itself to the changed conditions. What do we see instead of this? Immediately after the loss of the Chinese market became patent, there began the big capital expenditure of which the single purpose was to increase production far beyond the pre-war level. Once more we find the whole rationalization policy a mystery. What can the "leaders of industry" have had in mind when they inaugurated this great increase in production, at a time when any map of the world could have shown them that there was going to be a great fall in trade? We cannot believe that they had suddenly taken leave of their intelligence. Thus the loss of these markets only raises fresh problems, instead of bringing any solution. No vital raw material had been lost; it would have been perfectly possible—perhaps with a reduced level of prices—to get quite comfortably adjusted to the new situation. Why was it not done?

MORPHOLOGICAL EXPLANATION

We fear we must be beginning to tire the reader. It is always the same tale—the facts assigned as cause of the crisis by the various theories are all perfectly sound facts; only they are not the cause. Either they are themselves symptoms, if not actually effects of the crisis, even effects produced in the effort to combat it, though they then help to accentuate the symptoms through the law of action and reaction; or else they are intermediate causes which themselves require explanation and are themselves symptoms of a disorder, such as the oft-mentioned rationalization or the unequal distribution of gold. Throughout, the fundamental cause eludes us.

One may judge how utterly resigned the experts are already to failure to discover any such fundamental cause, from the fact that they have gone the length of abdicating in favour of an acceptance of the crisis as "morphological." The curve of the alternations of boom and slump has been traced for the past century and a half, and the pronouncement has been made that this wave-line is itself superposed on the underlying rhythm of "long waves." No cause of these "long waves" is known; they have been termed, in the biological style of a Spengler, "growth periods of world trade." We are to regard ourselves as caught in the descending curve of one of these long waves. The end of the shrinkage of trade, on this theory, and the beginning of a reversal of this fundamental movement is not to be expected until 1940—a sentence that does not exclude the possible mitigation of superposed short-wave peaks or "interim booms."

It may be so—but is that an explanation? Statistical science is the science of big figures, built up on the hypothesis that the arbitrariness of the single instance is eliminated by the frequency of its repetition. It seems to us that the number of crises of the capitalist system that our survey can comprehend is too small to enable us yet to deduce from them laws of this sort. As yet few crises have been comparable with one another—and we have already established that the present one is comparable with none of them.

That does not mean that the detection of long waves and "periods of growth" is necessarily of no scientific value. But for the attainment of knowledge in the field of human activity all that is the mere sweeping of the threshold. For the attainment of knowledge of the processes of Nature, who never bares her soul to humanity, it may be the height of methodical wisdom to begin by assuming "causes" to be a complete mystery, and to confine oneself to compiling a curve which is nothing more than an indication of the changes effected in the course of time. Man's economic activity, on the other hand, is our own activity, and here if anywhere every single step in his dealings proceeds from the coolest of intelligent calculation. Endless mistakes may be made, but they must be recognizable and intelligible to us.

Consequently we have not the slightest intention of confining ourselves, in our search for the explanation of the world crisis, to the study of a curve, as though it were enough to consider the temperature and the state of the barometer. Everything that has been done in world trade since the end of the War has been done by men and women, who reflected on what they were going to do, and who, it is safe to assume, were out to enrich themselves—that is a simple matter, and its sum total must be recognizable. We note, however, the attempt to give the crisis a morphological explanation as a symptom of the extent to which the experts have resigned themselves to failing ever to arrive at a knowledge of its fundamental causes.

Thus our examination of the causes so far assigned to the crisis ends with a negative result. If this were no more than a matter of the attainment of scientific knowledge, one might leave the doctors to disagree. But the situation becomes still more hopeless when one proceeds to consider the practical demands and remedies deduced from these causes.

THE GOOD GOD OF TRADE IN A FIX

Let us imagine for a moment that there is throned beyond the dark clouds of trade an omniscient Intelligence who has the power to influence the course of world trade as he will, just as the good god of the legends controls the weather. This god observed with compassion the unhappy lot of trading humanity and declared himself ready and anxious to send them better weather. Let them just send him their wise men, so that he might learn their desires. What sort of a story would he be likely to hear?

One counsellor would say: "You must get rid of over-production."

"No," a second would declare, "production has fallen quite enough; you must revive consumption."

The third: "You must put a curb on rationalization and stop the moving platform."

The fourth: "You must go right ahead with rationalization, in the backward countries, especially among the German agriculturists."

The fifth: "You must increase the production of gold."

The sixth: "That is quite unnecessary; you need only distribute the gold differently."

The seventh: "You must remove all price commitments as quickly as possible and restore the conditions of the free market."

"For God's sake," the next would exclaim, "don't! It would mean absolute chaos. The only thing that can help us is a 'sensible' cartel policy."

Yet another: "You must at once abrogate all protective tariffs."

His neighbour: "That would be actually to break down the sole barriers that have held off chaos up to now. You must shut off all the economic areas from one another."

Could anyone blame the good god if, in the end, he thundered: "I command the seed to fructify and the crops to ripen; that is all I have learnt to do. If men so contrive that they starve in the face of plenty, that is their doing"?

Chapter Four

THE SECOND QUESTION: WORLD INDEBTEDNESS

The examination of the familiar theories of the crisis has brought no satisfactory result. We have made the acquaintance of a collection of ideals all of which are quite ably thought out, but at the end we are as wise as before. That does not mean that all these theories are mistaken. On the contrary, we had the satisfaction of recognizing that most of them were actually sound, or at least "sound at the core," only they did not entirely meet the case. Most of them were sound in the sense in which it is undeniably a sound explanation of a motor-car accident that it was the force of gravity that sent the car down the declivity when it went over the edge of the road. Would that explanation meet people's everyday requirements? Only in science do we find explanations of that high order of logic. Gravity is at work all the time, but it cannot carry the car down the slope until it has lost its equilibrium by getting off the road. Similarly, economic laws are operative all the time, on good days equally with bad. But, after all, one cannot expect them to explain the good trade in good times and the bad trade in bad times. Most of the theories blandly took for granted a loss of equilibrium. The raising of tariff barriers implies a change from earlier conditions in the world market, a change from which the home market is to be guarded by protective dikes. Or, if rationalization is carried to such lengths that afterwards people are able to talk of ill-judged capital expenditure, it is understandable that it should bring trouble. Only, the question arises what it was that induced this excessive resort to rationalization. Sometimes we reminded ourselves irresistibly of a little child who goes on, as soon as Mamma has answered one question, to cap it with another "Why?" Still more negative was the result when we considered the practical conclusions to be drawn from the theories.

Some readers may object that along these lines one can reject any theory, for every theory leaves the path to a new "Why?" open. It is easy to see, they may allege, that our negative result is not disinterestedly arrived at; for if we allowed ourselves to be satisfied with any theory, we should have to stop writing this book. To meet that suspicion, let us bring forward one or two witnesses who share all our pessimism with regard to the economists' contributions to an explanation of the crisis. Two witnesses may suffice—it would be easy to add to their number. We shall deliberately choose two liberal writers as our witnesses, because the liberals are the most ready to put faith in the economists. In the *Vossische Zeitung* of September 13, 1931 Richard Winners summarizes the result of a consideration of the latest literature on the economic crisis as follows: "What does it all come to? Nothing or next to nothing; for the answer furnished by each expert would be a different one. Opinions differ entirely on what is needed to combat the crisis. No common program can be got out of the multiplicity of views, so that there is very little assistance towards a practical economic policy to be gathered from the advice of the experts." And in the *Berliner Tageblatt* of August 30, 1931 Theodor Wolff, of whom even his opponents will allow at least that he is acquainted with the literature of the subject, writes: "Amid all the plans brought forward today for the healing of our economic troubles, one can only sadly reflect that it is precisely in Germany and England that since the beginning of modern times there has been a flourishing science called political economy. And after all the immense expenditure of learning and acumen we have not yet, in the year 1931, got beyond the most primitive of devices; the delicate instruments invented by the experts are left unutilized in favour of the kitchen rolling-pin. Any counting-house apprentice on his stool can calculate how much is brought in by raising a tax and cutting wages ten or twenty per cent. Why do people study political economy?"

To say that a whole science, represented by so much intelligence, has failed may be a harsh verdict. But think, by way of comparison, what medicine, for instance, has done in the combating of sleeping-sickness; will anyone venture to claim that political economy has anything to its credit in combating the world sickness of the crisis that is comparable with such achievements as that? The economic experts may as well candidly admit it—they were just as much taken by surprise by the outbreak of the crisis as they were in 1914 by the outbreak of the World War. And the failure this time is much worse, for in 1914 the course of events depended much more largely on irrational personal decisions. The crisis, on the contrary, came with such inexorable logical necessity as not much else could; yet nobody saw it coming. (As lately as the middle of 1930 Kurt Singer, in an article headed *"Weltwirtschafts-Krisis?"*—in *Wirtschaftsdienst,* No. 33 of 1930—endowed the world economic crisis with a note of interrogation and demonstrated on the basis of practical economic considerations that there was no justification for talking of a world crisis.) Once the economic disease had broken out, should it not have gone without saying that, if only under the urge to pursue knowledge, the experts would have no peace until they had assembled from all countries in a Council of Scientists, that should have no thought of dissolving until the disease had been identified and the right therapy discovered—in the service of humanity and to the greater glory of science? Instead, everyone is setting up any causes to his taste, *a posteriori,* and defending them against all comers, blind to the ironic fact that even if he is right, there is nothing in it: he should have recognized the workings of these causes of his and given warning of them in advance, and then he would have achieved something.

The German nationalists will repudiate any such charge: they will declare that they "always prophesied it." But they prophesied only within the framework of their purely German outlook; they predicted the German crisis and demanded accordingly a short and sharp foreign policy; they did not predict the world crisis. Did they predict that world market prices would fall thirty per cent within two and a half years? And even if they had done, would they not have been much wiser to demand that Germany should hold her hand for a little while, since a fall in prices on that scale is a much healthier cure for the creditor powers than any policy of protest from unarmed Germany?

The American reader will not be surprised at this sceptical estimate of political economy and the political economists. There has been published in the United States (after the German original of this book appeared) the entertaining book *Oh Yeah?* in which all the prophesyings of the economic experts on the economic situation which have since been so bitterly refuted by the course of the crisis are collected with merciless cruelty. It is recalled, for instance, how as lately as December 1929 a leading bank announced in its monthly report that "There have been no important bankruptcies and none are to be expected," etc. The book enables one to appreciate why it is that the most famous economic experts have given up prophesying.

THE SPECIAL FEATURE OF POST-WAR TRADE

Let us forget, then, all that we learned in the last chapter of the views of the political economists. Let us ask, quite naïvely, why everything should be going so much worse today in all the countries of the world than in the "normal year" 1913, which to this day is instinctively taken as normal by the economists in all their calculations of index numbers. When the War was over, all the world hoped that pre-war conditions would soon be restored. And in all the talk of "reconstruction" there was an unexpressed central idea that a system of trade and industry must be organized that would function as the pre-war system functioned. Why is this work of rebuilding, after thirteen years, still failing, why do we feel today farther from success than ever? The world is like a trunk of which the contents were brutally turned upside down by the War, and now no amount of pains will make it repack so as to shut again. Why not? What is it that distinguishes the world of today from the pre-war world?

Obviously, the fact that we are a post-war world, that the effects of the War are still present. Is that to be our answer? In the period that has since elapsed, the war-time destruction of goods has been amply made good, the stocks have been replenished, the machinery renewed, and the apparatus of production is functioning decidedly better than before the War. In all this there is no longer any trace of the War to be found.

But in the world's account-books the War is still very much with us. There it stands entered as the debts remaining over from the War. For the belligerent States waged the War at the expense of the future.

No man can contest the statement that the post-war economic life is distinguished from the pre-war economic life by the fact that it is burdened in advance with the debts of the War.

Let us see what this means to trade and industry. Let us forget meanwhile all about the crisis. Let us simply consider how an economic system so burdened in advance will function.

And let us remember once more that we do not want to think from a German point of view, but from that of world trade. Now that we are entering the field of the payments of the cost of the War, it is doubly important to keep that in mind. For the view that the world's economic perplexities have something to do with the world's debts was first expressed with no little emotion by those whom one might expect to express it, those whose money is in question. The question that we are now approaching has long been answered by the nationalist parties in Germany, and anyone who is content with their reply will have difficulty in understanding why we are making so many bones about it and attaching so much importance to establishing it.

In defence of keeping all that feeling out of our reply, let us point out that so far the German nationalist parties have not had the slightest success in convincing the world of the soundness of their logic. We will recall the account we gave in the first chapter of the current view of the liberal economists, that the Reparation payments have nothing whatever to do with the world crisis; we will recall once more the question put by Mr. Houghton and Mr. Strawn. If the nationalists reply that the world is not listening to them because the world "does not want to hear the truth," one has to point out that their statements offer no answer to Houghton's and Strawn's question. No nationalist political economist has yet succeeded in demonstrating a connexion between Reparations and the world crisis, because all their arguments stop short. They rightly contend that the Reparation payments withdraw purchasing power from Germany, and that the world market goes short of this purchasing power. But the question arises at once, why do not the creditor countries gain the purchasing power that Germany loses? If the creditor countries gain as much purchasing power as Germany loses, does not the sum of purchasing power in the world remain unaltered? Can it be that the creditor countries have reached a condition in which they can consume no more, because no one can eat more than his fill, because an American cannot buy more motor cars than one for himself and one for his wife and one for each of the "juniors"? But we are witnessing quite the reverse of this, we see the American obliged to cut down his consumption, and the always optimistic Mr. Ford compelled to reduce output. All these questions are left unanswered by the nationalist economists. They are less answered than ever when emotion takes the place of logic—however noble the emotion. We want to deal with the question of the effects of the war-debt payments perfectly coolly, as though it were some other people that had to make the payments.

DALBERG'S THEORY

An inquiry into this question, as unimpassioned and strictly scientific as we have postulated, was published a year ago by Herr Dalberg in his "*Weltkrise, Goldproblem und Kriegsschulden* (World Crisis, Gold Problem, and War Debts)"—in No. 31 of the *Bankarchiv*, August 30, 1930).

Dalberg makes the Strakosch theory the starting-point of his work. We will recall that Strakosch seeks to attribute the slump in prices to monetary causes. In consequence, he argues, of the unequal distribution of gold, part of the gold is sterilized: gold on which no credit is built up is no longer fulfilling any monetary function.

Dalberg agrees with us in finding these ideas quite sound. But he goes on, and rightly, to object that Strakosch did not carry his ideas to their logical conclusion. What is the cause of the unequal distribution of gold? For it is not itself a final cause, but a result of other causes.

The flow of gold to the note banks of America and France is, to begin with, the expression of a credit balance of international payments. The principal cause of this credit balance is the war-debt payments. For these payments are not *at once* returned to the debtor countries either in the form of consumption or in that of credits or capital investment. "Failing such rapid and complete clearing of payments, there will remain balances unsettled, which will then be paid in gold. Such misconsignments of gold to centres which have no need of gold are simply consequences of the system of political debts which the World War left behind it. It is in the political payments made from country to country, to an annual amount of two milliards of marks, that the final causes of the world crisis lie."

Dalberg is well aware that there is no need of Strakosch's gold theory for the formulation of this interrelationship. He knows that, as we showed above, the gold theory is only a cover, a means of expression, of which use may be made or not at will, without altering the fact which it covers. The interrelationship can be formulated without talking in terms of gold. We quote again from Dalberg: "With her purchasing power weakened by political debts and not fully restored by an adequate re-supply of capital, Germany fell to some extent out of the world market as buyer of raw materials (in spite of figures which in themselves are high). In this fact lies the fundamental impulse towards the slump in prices all over the world. But, once the downward movement in prices had begun, it was bound to continue by a sort of wave-motion; for the purchasing power of the raw-material producers in the U.S.A. and the British Empire fell, with resulting reduction of output and falling purchasing power of the working masses in these branches of production; and the rapid repercussion of this on the economic fields at first unaffected has produced the spectacle of the present world depression." Dalberg's formulation of these ideas eighteen months ago was an achievement. Today they have been so often repeated in the newspapers that they have become too hackneyed to be exciting in Germany any longer. But does that prove them right? Dalberg adduces for an effect of definite magnitude, the slump in world prices, a cause of definite magnitude, the political payments. "Thus the tying up of two milliards of political debts has cost the world in a single year many dozens of milliards in reduced production." How does this small cause produce this multifold effect? How is one to conceive the mechanism by which a cause so multiplies itself in a single year? Dalberg has left that question unanswered.

Thus we are faced once more with Mr. Houghton's question.

Let us re-read Dalberg's statements, to see whether this acute writer has not after all observed that there is a yawning gap here in his argument. For this author is far above any suspicion of exaggerating the effects of Reparations to score a point, or of letting his fancy run away with him. He writes, in so many words: "With her purchasing power weakened by political debts . . . Germany fell to some extent out of the world market as buyer. . . . In this fact lies the fundamental impulse towards the slump in prices all over the world." It will be seen that the means by which Dalberg skims over the question of the relative magnitude of cause and effect is the phrase "fundamental impulse." A "fundamental" impulse is nothing at all; the essence of an impulse is that it does not itself supply the energy for movement, but is a mere impulse. If an impulse makes a truck move, the gradient and the force of gravity account for its continuing to move; on a horizontal plane it will soon come to a stop. An impulse does no more than overcome an initial resistance; the actual movement is maintained from some other source of energy and continues even if the force of the impulse itself has long been exhausted. But probably that is not what Dalberg means; he must surely mean that if the German obligations to pay were removed, the world crisis would gradually come to a stop.—The other statement, that the downward movement in prices continues "by a sort of wave-motion," is not an explanation.

Or is Dalberg's idea that the action of the Reparation payments is something comparable to that of the amplifier in wireless transmission—that they determine only the form and phase of the economic wave-motion, while the magnitude of the effect is determined by the additional energy of the amplifier? In that case, where would the additional energy come from? We are offered no explanation.

So we must try to pursue our line of thought alone.

REPARATIONS AND DEBT SERVICE

The point from which Dalberg and all the economic theoreticians proceed in their search for the connexion between war-debt payments and the world crisis is contained in Dalberg's statement that "When, through the war-debt payments, a round two milliards are paid annually by Germany to the creditor countries, that means a loss of purchasing power for the debtor country and a corresponding increase in purchasing power for the creditor countries." That statement is entirely correct as far as it goes, but it does not go far enough. For in that case the net purchasing power of the world would remain unaltered. The question is whether the newly won purchasing power of the creditor countries is applied directly to the market, or, if not, by what indirect means.

If one thinks only in terms of regional economic groups, one fails to approach the problem. Viewed so, all that there is to be seen is the transfer from one economic body to another. Where is there in that case a point of application at which a crisis-producing mechanism could operate?

One must look from closer up, and follow the course actually taken by particular debt payments.

The payments received by the creditor States are not simply hoarded, and while it is true that the gold reserves in the vaults of their banks mount up, this only happens after manifold manipulations and because no other way is possible of clearing the credit balance of payments.

The payments received are employed first in the service of the internal debt. The State did not get the money with which it waged war, or which it lent to its allies, from the exchequer, but first borrowed it from the citizens of its country. Now it repays them. What does that mean?

People are tempted to reply that this is entirely beside the question under consideration, that of world purchasing power and the world crisis. The only thing that matters is that money paid out on account of internal debts remains within the country. External debts reduce a country's purchasing power, internal ones leave it unchanged—in that simple dictum the question seems to be answered.

But we Germans have had experience of the formula that in the case of internal debt "the money remains within the country." This formula was used to make the internal indebtedness through the war loans palatable to us; we were told that Germany's economic system would win over against those of the enemy States, which were borrowing abroad. In our case the money remained within the country; but in spite of that it happened that the increased pace of war-time circulation brought a great transfer of incomes and of property. On the one side the war profiteers grew rich; on the other, in spite of increased wages, the masses suffered from the increase in prices, quite apart from the millions of those who had to be content with the wages of the simple soldier. Thus, by taking money in the form of war loans and giving it out in the form of war contracts and wage payments, the State succeeded in producing a great transfer of income, although the money remained within the country: accumulation of fortunes on the one side; on the other, reduction of consumption owing to increased prices.

This very familiar story is only recalled by way of illustration. It should point the moral that, if the money remains within the country, that is far from guaranteeing that there will not, for all that, be a shifting of income levels under which the consuming power of the masses declines.

In order to attain clearness on this point, we will consider, purely in theory, what is the effect of internal loans on a country's economic system.

THE ECONOMIC EFFECT OF INTERNAL DEBTS

The classic origin of public borrowing on the modern scale was provided, of course, by the railways. The fiscal science of the eighteenth century had always regarded State debts with mixed feelings. They were regarded as in no way differing from private debts, which always carried a suggestion of imperfect morality and which it was only respectable to repay as soon as possible. When, in the France of the Revolution, the State debts had reached a total of three and a half milliards of francs, it was an unheard-of event and a proof of the demoralization of revolutionary administration. About 1800 the State debts of England, the most heavily indebted country, amounted to 465,000,000 pounds; in France to 800,000,000 francs, in Prussia in 1806 to 160,000,000 marks.

Not until the forties, when railway construction was beginning, did new views come with regard to State debts. It was recognized that it was possible for the productive forces of a country to grow in spite of the increase in the State debts, in so far as loans were productively applied.

When a State takes up a loan in order to build railways or set up any other economically productive plant, providing for interest and amortisation out of the yield of the enterprise, it is working no differently from any private entrepreneur. It is conceivable that the loan and its service might be kept as a separate account within the State budget, in no way affecting the rest of the budget. The interest and amortisation of the loan would be provided out of the return from the investment, the rest of the finances of the State remaining unaffected. The income of the mass of the population would similarly be unaffected by the service of the loan. The national income as a whole would be likely to be changed through the effects of the railway, but not through the actual service of the debt and not by the State as administrator of the debt.

If, on the other hand, a State takes up a loan of which the value is not invested for an economically productive purpose, but applied, say, to laying out parks and ornamental grounds, or to building a hospital to which the people will be admitted without charge, the interest and amortisation of the loan must then be met from the general revenues of the State—that is, from taxes and duties. It may conceivably be met from credits with a foreign State, but let us leave this last case out of consideration for the present and devote ourselves to that of the self-contained national economy. If the internal indebtedness of the State is increased without any corresponding increase in the productivity of the national economic system, and without the yield from customs and taxation increasing in the same degree, there remains no other course than for the State to increase the share of the national income which it claims in the form of taxes and duties. That means that the State is compelled to make a change in the distribution of the national income.

We come thus to the following propositions:

I. Internal indebtedness means liability to internal creditors; consequently, an increase in the internal indebtedness means:

a. If the loan is productively applied and the invested sums pay for their own amortisation, no change in the State budget and accordingly no State interference with the distribution of income. There may be an increase in the national wealth if in consequence of the investments the productivity of the country's economic system is increased.

b. If the loan is unproductively employed, compulsion to increase the State revenues from taxes and duties, and accordingly a change in the distribution of income.

For the sake of clearness the effect of external indebtedness may be given here:

II. External indebtedness means liability to the foreigner; consequently an increase in the external indebtedness means:

a. If the loan is unproductively employed, a diminution in any case in the national income and the national wealth;

b. If the loan is productively employed, this diminution can, if all goes well, be set off, or more than set off, by the yield obtained from the capital expenditure, so that the national wealth may conceivably increase.

There remains the case of which we deferred consideration, of internal debts amortised from foreign credit balances. We may confine ourselves to the case in which the credit balances belong to the State.

State credit balances abroad mean State revenues. If they came into existence through the State having first taken the money in question from its internal creditors and then handed it to the foreign debtor, the State exchequer is merely a channel for the interest paid by the foreign debtor, which it passes on to the other creditors. The effect that this has on national wealth and national income depends on the relative rates of interest. If they are absolutely equal, the State would earn nothing, and no one would be the gainer except the few officials occupied with the service of the debt. If the debtor's interest is the higher, the State is making a deal that may benefit the community through an increase in the State revenues and consequently a possible relief from taxation. If the interest paid to the creditors is the higher, the State must obtain the difference by taxation, which is paid by the community for the benefit of the creditors. That means that it comes to the same as if there existed merely an internal debt of the amount of the capital corresponding to the difference in interest: the effect is the same as that of any internal loan, and depends on whether it is productively or unproductively employed.

So far as war debts are concerned, the War, regarded from the point of view of world trade, certainly produced no increase in world productivity, but brought an enormous destruction of values. The debts contracted on account of the War must therefore, from the point of view of world trade, be regarded as unproductive debts. Of these, no one will have any hesitation in agreeing that the external debts mean a reduction of the purchasing power of the debtor national economic system. That does not mean that the internal debts can be left out of account from the point of view of world trade. They mean a shifting of income, with all the economic results that that entails.

Let not this statement be confused with the brutal fact that since the War some have grown poorer and others richer, that fortunes have been lost and others made. We are not thinking of private recipients of income, but of world trade.

If it were only that the State takes from one and gives to another, with no resultant change in the nature of the distribution of income or the *grading* of incomes, the shifting of incomes would have no effect on purchasing power.

But it is not so; the shifting of income effected by the debt service is at the same time a change in the *nature* of the income: the total of the incomes from labour is reduced and the total of the incomes from interest increased.

All this is no new discovery. But this line of thought is rather remote from the German layman. Germany's internal war debts were extinguished by the inflation, and accordingly the German's first thought when war debts are mentioned is of external debt. It does not occur to him that, if the Ruhr experiment had not been made and Germany had still her internal debt, she would be having to pass now through an incomparably worse crisis, or might long ago have had openly to declare the State bankruptcy which she suffered in a disguised form through the inflation, together with the exiguous revaluation of securities which was afterwards enacted.

In making the foregoing remarks we do not want to lay ourselves open to the charge of entertaining the foolish idea that the German people became one pfennig the richer by the extinction of the internal war debt. All that has happened is that we have been spared a crisis in income-distribution.

The fallacy just mentioned is regularly brought up, especially by the French press. Again and again French writers maintain in entire earnest that the extinction of Germany's war debts, which, of course, were entirely internal debts, has correspondingly increased her capacity to pay. We should not mention this if this habit of putting internal and external debts on a par were confined to the French layman and were not continually being indulged in by the most prominent French statesmen.

While Germans and French, each after his own fashion, tend to forget the distinction between internal and external debt, the whole world is one in its incapacity to keep in mind the distinction between productive and unproductive employment of public loans. America especially, who came straight into a world of labouring citizens, who never knew the princes who raised loans in order to give money to their mistresses, and never had to plumb the mysteries of the fiscal science of the eighteenth century, has never bethought herself of the danger of treating all State loans alike, irrespective of the purpose to which they are to be applied. It has never occurred to her that the State could apply loans unproductively. State loans are absolutely safe because the State backs them with its authority. It has never occurred, however, to the Americans that State loans have quite different effects on the national economic life from those of private loans.

Private loans can never produce a regrading of incomes within the community when they are employed for unproductive purposes. In such cases they disappear; the debtor must sacrifice an equivalent part of his property or go bankrupt. Only the State can provide the interest and amortisation of unproductive loans, as it has the national economic system itself as "assets" on which it can draw. In this way, thanks to the authority of the State, unproductive loans are raised, and interest and amortisation paid on them, in cases in which by any rule of private business the capital would long ago have been lost. All this does not exclude the possibility that this may exactly fit the secret history of State borrowings for railway construction.

THE ORDER OF MAGNITUDE OF WORLD INDEBTEDNESS

So far we have kept to pure theory. Has the shifting of incomes which we have theoretically argued taken place in fact in the creditor countries? No statistics of incomes in the creditor countries are to be had in such a form as to enable us directly to trace this shifting. It is evidenced indirectly by the fall in consuming power which traders are bewailing, and the fall in taxation yield which is bewailed by ministers of finance.

Indirect evidence, however, is not entirely conclusive. The fall in purchasing power and in taxation yield might have other causes. We must try, therefore, to ascertain by some other means the extent of the shifting of incomes effected by internal debt service.

The extent of this shifting of incomes will depend on the two following factors:

1. On the ratio of internal indebtedness to national wealth, or on that taken together with the ratio of the State debt service to the State budget.
2. On the economic situation of the loanholders; in other words, on the hands into which the war loan has come.

On the latter point we have no exact particulars. Two extreme cases are conceivable: Let us assume that the war loans were taken up in the creditor countries to an equal amount by every recipient of an income—a case which would virtually occur if, for instance, the loan had been raised through a compulsory poll-tax. In such a case the interest on the loan would go precisely to those who had to pay the taxes for the debt service. The amount of the tax would simply be reduced by that of the interest.

As another extreme case, assume that the whole of the war loans were subscribed by one individual Rothschild. The whole of the money for the debt service would then flow into the pockets of a single man.

The actual position must lie between these two extreme cases.

Now, in order to gauge the actual position in America, which primarily interests us here, America being the principal creditor of the world, it must be borne in mind that the American Liberty Loans were never "national loans" in the sense of the later German war loans. They were not for the simple reason that the American economic system was never squeezed as dry as the German was in the later years of the War. Within the American economic system the war loans fulfilled quite another function. The bulk of the consideration for these loans went to the United States in the form of credits for goods, which were then realized in the United States themselves through the purchase of goods. Thus, with the money produced by the issue of the loan, the American Government opened credits for goods for the Allied Powers, the Allies paid by depositing their treasury bills with the United States Treasury, and the Government paid the producers of the goods the money that it had obtained on loan. The whole proceeding was thus conducted on the basis of a credit granted by American private capitalists to the European countries, the American Government undertaking the guarantee of the interest (and a good high rate of interest) and amortisation. Mr. Mellon himself described the process unambiguously to the president of Princeton University in his letter of March 15, 1927: "When we came into the War we agreed to furnish our Associates the dollars with which all their purchases in the United States should be consummated and, what is more, we agreed to lend them those dollars. *This was the origin of these debts.*"

These transactions, as we said, were essentially a granting of credit by private capital under a State guarantee; the mass of the American people had relatively little part in them. In the course of the War these credits for goods reached a total of 42,000,000,000 gold marks. The guarantee into which it entered cost the American Government a great deal of money. It has had to pay annually to capitalists in the United States some 1,800,000,000 gold marks. The European debtors, on the other hand, paid very badly. In the three years 1919–21 they paid altogether some 879,000,000 gold marks, or less than half of one year's interest. This disproportion gave Congress the energy in 1922 to set up the well-known Debt Commission, to take in hand the settlement of the American claims on foreign countries.

These familiar things are recalled here only to make plain to the German reader the difference between the economic function of the American and of the German war loans. It is useless to argue from the distribution of the German loan paper—mostly among the German middle class, since defunct—to the holders of the American loans.

So much for the second of the two points mentioned

above. The first, the relative magnitude of the war debts, must occupy us at more length. In discussing this we shall reply at the same time to an objection which probably has for some time been in the minds of many readers: that there is nothing "new in principle" in the World War having been carried on at the expense of the future. Since the rise of modern credit methods wars have regularly been waged on credit, and the history of modern credit would be unrecognizable with the financing of war left unmentioned. Court bankers were, above all, war bankers. Why, then, make such a song about war indebtedness when it is certainly no new thing in history?

But political economy is concerned with the relations of economic *magnitudes*. It is never a question of the principle, everything is as old as the hills, the only things that matter and are new are the magnitudes. Past generations may have thought the burdens of debt left by earlier wars just as oppressive as the present burdens seem to us, but that makes no difference to the fact that never before in world history have the States of half the world mobilized a sum that represents a substantial portion of their national wealth. Never has that occurred before, and never has an international plan of payments spread over two generations been elaborated and adopted.

The figures themselves will best show that we are dealing this time with sums of quite a different order of magnitude. The whole war of 1870, lasting 245 days, cost Prussia, including all costs of reconstruction, no more than 3,500,000,000 marks. It cost France, including all costs of reconstruction and the cost of maintenance of the Prussian army, actually a little less, 3,400,000,000 marks. (On top of that there was the war indemnity of 4,050,000,000 marks.) Let it not be objected that that is far away in the past. The Russo-Japanese war of 1904–5, waged entirely by modern methods of war, and lasting a year and a half, (550 days), cost Russia 2,900,000,000 marks and Japan 2,400,000,000 marks (Helfferich's calculation). Will anyone try to persuade us that it is really nothing "new in principle" if these figures are multiplied by one hundred or two hundred? If in 1913 a political economist had ventured to prophesy that the world was going to have a war of which the cost would exceed one thousand milliards, a million millions of gold marks, would not the man have been declared insane? Would not all the economic experts have cried with one voice: "Impossible"? What can have happened since then to enable the economic system to bear an expenditure of an order of magnitude hitherto inconceivable?

Woytinski has calculated the total expenditure of the War of all the countries that took part in it to be 1,040,000,000,000 gold marks. From this have to be deducted the double entries due to the war loans made to one another by the belligerent nations, and also the depreciation of money which set in during the War. This brings the total cost of the War down to 700,000,000,000 gold marks. Of this sum only one sixth, or seventeen per cent (120,000,000,000) was raised by taxation during the War. That as much as this was actually paid during the War is mainly to the credit of the very conscientious British financial administration. Throughout the War the British feeling had been that it was a duty to pay for the War as far as possible in cash. The British taxation was continually increased, at the risk of making the War unpopular. Yet Britain was unable to raise more than 50,000,000,000 gold marks, less than thirty per cent of her war expenditure, by taxation. The United States raised 44,300,000,000 gold marks by taxation during the War, and Germany only 15,300,000,000.

The whole of the rest of the expenditure on the War—five sixths, or eighty-three per cent, in all 580,000,000,000 gold marks—was incurred by the belligerent world "on tick," and the payment for it left to the future. How did it suppose the future was going to pay?

The figures are too vast for comprehension. The picture becomes just a little more within one's imaginative grasp if one takes the budgets of the individual belligerent States. When Great Britain went into the War, in 1914, she had a State debt of 706,000,000 pounds. When the War ended, in 1919, the State debt had grown to 7,481,000,000 pounds, and in the following year, owing to the funding of floating debt, it rose to 7,875,000,000 pounds. Thus in the war years the national debt had been multiplied by eleven. The United States had a State debt of 1,180,000,000 dollars; at the end of the War, in 1919, the debt had grown to 25,480,000,000—actually multiplied twenty times. The situation of France and Italy would be similarly serious if they had not been assisted by a measure of inflation.

What have the peoples actually thought about this multiplication of debts which they have achieved for the delight of coming generations? Probably nothing at all—they have simply become used to the figures. They have applied the rules of addition and multiplication that they learned in the elementary school, and have felt sure that the figures were all right, so long as they were correctly calculated. The German inflation showed the apparently illimitable capacity of people to get used to figures.

But one must not expect people who take the figures as they come to realize that in truth there are very real limits, that real things cannot be simply multiplied like numerals on a sheet of paper, but in real life, with the passage to another order of magnitude, something quite different comes into being. A row of figures is something continuous, it is always possible to add to it and multiply it, there is no sudden jump. Why should it not be possible to multiply war debts in the same way? If the last war cost hundreds of milliards, why should not the next one cost thousands? One has to get beyond the field of arithmetic to understand that. Biology knows more about the relations between size and life. An ichthyosaurus is a multiplied lizard, but the lizard still lives, the ichthyosaurus has died. One may picture to oneself a blade of grass as tall as a forest tree, but in reality it would be unable to live. Nature made the attempt to grow a horsetail (equisetum) as big as a forest tree, but the horsetail woods died out, and Nature abandoned the experiment. Will the ichthyosaurus of war debts be able to live? Or is it doomed to a premature death?

But we will try to get a better conception of the limits that are set to the multiplicability of unproductive debts in the real world of economic life than a mere simile can give.

The only possible source of the interest and amortisation of war loans is the yield of the productive economic activities of the world. War loans themselves produce nothing. They have been spent unproductively, *verpufft*—spent on a bang and a puff of smoke. The munitions have been shot off, the material destroyed and squandered, the wages eaten up. That ends that. The productively working capital of world trade and industry must struggle through with the dead weight of that item on its shoulders. There is nothing else for it.

If it has been possible for the war debts arising from the wars of the past to be paid off in subsequent years, it has been only because those debts, in proportion to the productively working capital of the economic system concerned, were small enough for it to digest. We have seen how relatively small they were. The debts arising from the last war are beyond all comparison with any other. There is thus no useful purpose to be served by bringing up the history of the payment of the debts left by earlier wars. There is nothing that we can learn from it.

But if the dead weight of unproductive war loans is too much for the productive capital to bear, if the debts are more than it can digest, what happens then?

Then trade and industry help themselves. They go on, so surely as men will feel the approach of hunger and will work to still it. The capacity for self-help of the economic system is extraordinary. The only question is whether it will go steadily ahead or help itself by the remedy of catastrophes.

A few of these catastrophes, by means of which the economic system has purged itself of a part of its indigestible debts, have occurred already. We gave above the amount of the war expenditure met by the raising of loans—580,000,000,000 gold marks (external and internal debts together). Of this amount the lesser half has already been written off through the collapse of the Central Powers and the German inflation. Germany has provided a demonstration of what happens in practice to the sum that one may multiply indefinitely on paper. She has shown that by multiplication one can go on producing values on paper until they destroy themselves. The other powers have not carried multiplication so far, but it must not be inferred that they have completely funded their debt scores. A further amount was got rid of by Russia's farewell to Western civilization and her retirement from the complexities of the world credit system.

When the negotiations for the settlement of the interallied debts began, in 1924, there was down for discussion a sum of 87,000,000,000 gold marks of *external* debt. Of this amount a net 49,500,000,000 was due to the United States; Great Britain was owed 30,200,000,000, and herself owed 19,200,000,000 to the United States; France was owed 7,000,000,000, and herself owed 30,200,000,000 to the United States and Great Britain; Italy had debts of 21,000,000,000 against a credit of only 300,000,000—all in gold marks. But it very soon became clear that there was no conceivable possibility of getting in even these 87,000,000,000 gold marks.

We shall not subject the reader to yet another of the countless narratives of the complicated course of the debt agreements. We need only recall briefly what happened in the end to these 87,000,000,000 gold marks. America held fast, on paper, to the total of her credit: adding together the "funding totals" which were taken as the basis of the agreements with the various debtor States, one arrives at the final total of 12,036,000,000 dollars. The actual concessions were made, of course, in rate of interest and period allowed for repayment. The Commission had been given strict marching orders by Congress: the debt must be cleared within twenty-five years, and the interest must not be less than four and a half per cent. When the agreements were completed, the period of repayment had grown to sixty-two years; the interest was specially agreed with each debtor, and here it must be admitted that America showed extraordinary leniency. France, for instance, paid no interest whatever in the first five years; interest then came into play, rising very slowly to a maximum of three and a half per cent, which does not become payable until 1965. Signor Mussolini succeeded in obtaining even better terms: Italy also paid no interest for the first five years; the interest is then one eighth per cent from 1930 to 1940; then it increases slowly up to one per cent, and not until the last seven years does it reach the maximum of two per cent. Even the strongest of the debtors, Great Britain, pays only three per cent during the first ten years, and thereafter the maximum of three and a half per cent. That is all that is left of the marching orders of Congress.

Capitalizing these agreements at an average interest of four and a half per cent, one gets a cash value of 6,860,000,000 dollars. Half of the credit has thus melted away.

Great Britain went even further to meet her debtors. Out of her credit of 30,200,000,000 gold marks the agreements left a present value of 11,000,000,000.

Thus the 87,000,000,000 of the interallied external debts were brought down, at the 1925 valuation, to a capital value of some 37,000,000,000 gold marks.

That sounds very handsome, when one remembers the original amount of the cost of the War. But if one reflects that these 37,000,000,000 gold marks are unproductive debts, that their interest and amortisation have to be found, not out of the economic yield of the investment of these 37,000,000,000, but out of the yield from the world's really productive capital, one realizes with alarm the enormous dead weight on world trade and industry that they make. It is scarcely necessary to mention that virtually the whole of this dead weight is shifted on to the trade and industry of Germany.

Even so, if these 37,000,000,000 were the whole of the burden, they might not be too much for world trade to bear. Then the situation would be as the creditor powers imagined it amid their calculations: Germany would be crippled by the burden of her obligations, but the other national economic systems would be flourishing so much the more. But the 37,000,000,000 were only what was left of the 87,000,000,000 of external debt. If we want to grasp the full measure of the dead weight on the world's trade, we must not forget the internal indebtedness.

INTERNAL INDEBTEDNESS IN PARTICULAR

All debt payments end with the creditor within the country. External debt is built up on internal. The State has no money, it can only lend out what it has itself borrowed. Thus it is on the use that the internal creditor makes of the moneys which he receives from the repayments of external debts that the effect of these repayments from country to country depends.

But that by no means exhausts the significance of internal debts. As we saw, the internal debts incurred during the War for the payment of its cost were many times greater than the external debts. Of the 580,000,000,000 of gold marks of war debt only 100,000,000,000 were external debts, and the remaining 480,000,000,000 internal. What has happened to these 480,000,000,000?

As we have already mentioned, a considerable part melted away through inflation: the whole in Germany and Austria, three quarters or four fifths in France, Belgium, and Italy. In the countries, however, that have kept their currencies up to pre-war, the internal debt still stands at its full value. The following table shows the position of the internal debts of the countries which did most of the financing of the war on the victors' side, for the years 1914, 1920, 1925, and 1929. For the sake of clearness the external and total debts are also shown.

This summary shows, to begin with, how much greater the internal debts are than the external. America has, of course, only internal debts; but in Great Britain the internal debts are six times the amount of the other. The States which have gone through a measure of inflation come out much better. In France in 1929 the internal debts were little more than one and a half times the external, in Italy only one and two fifths times.

These internal debts have no influence on the national wealth of the country concerned, but in

Internal and External Debt of Certain States
(In milliards of the national currency)

		1914	*1920*	*1925*	*1929*
Great Britain					
Internal ..	£	0.706	6.6	6.52	6.51
External ..	£	.....	1.2	1.12	1.08
Total ..	£	0.706	7.8	7.64	7.59
France					
Internal ..	francs	34.1	202.5	286.4	265.0
External ..	"	.....	83.3	138.6	169.4
Total ..	"	34.1	285.8	425.0	434.4
Italy					
Internal ..	lire	15.7	74.5	90.8	87.1
External ..	"	.....	78.9	128.6	64.7
Total ..	"	15.7	153.5	219.4	151.8
United States					
Internal ..	$	1.18	24.3	20.5	16.9
External ..	$	.....	....	.....	.....
Total ..	$	1.18	24.3	20.5	16.9

regard to the national income, as we showed at excessive length, they effect a shifting. Viewed, however, from the standpoint of the productivity of the world's capital, they are just as much of a dead weight as the external debts. The capital so invested has been just as unproductively squandered as the external loans; it, too, has been shot into the air and produces nothing more.

Now, in proceeding to calculate the magnitude of the total burden that is draining the energies of the world's economic system by its demand for interest and amortisation, although it is itself producing nothing, it will not do simply to add together internal and external debt. As we have pointed out, the payment that a debtor State makes in its external debt service is not retained by the creditor State, but is passed on at once to its internal creditors. Thus, in the internal debts of the creditor State we count over again the external debts of the debtor State. It is therefore sufficient if we add together the internal debts of the principal creditor States on the side of the victors. The War was, indeed, financed only by a few great capitalist States; the lesser Allies paid all their expenses by external borrowing. The calculation works out roughly as follows (position in 1929):

	Millard gold marks
United States	70.9
Great Britain	132.6
France	53.0
Italy	21.8
Belgium	4.9
Total	283.2

The figure is appalling. The final total would, moreover, have been much greater if we had taken the position in 1919. But we are not concerned to give a historical account of the cost of the War, but to get a fairly recent figure for the present dead weight on trade and industry—the figure, be it observed, for the year in which the crisis began.

Is there no way of reducing this appallingly high figure? One possibility of subtraction offers itself. We want to get only the unproductive war debts. We must therefore deduct the pre-war internal debts. For, before the War, States normally incurred internal debts only for productive purposes or for so-called cultural expenditure. But what does this deduction amount to?

	Millard gold marks
United States	4·95
Great Britain	14·19
France	27·5
Italy	17·4
Belgium	3·3
Total	67·34

Since the War the various States have incurred further debts for productive purposes, though on a relatively small scale. But the calculation gives no better result if we take the 1919 figures instead of those for 1929. On the contrary, as we have just said, they would come substantially higher; for the amortisation of the internal debts during the period 1919–29 considerably exceeds the amount of the further borrowing. Let us take a wide margin and deduct for productive internal loans since the War the round sum of 5,000,000,000 gold marks; the fact remains that in 1929 there was still left an internal debt burden of some 210,000,000,000 gold marks. This figure should be right as a rough approximation.

Thus in 1929, eleven years after the end of the World War, the War still stood in the books of the world's trade as a dead weight of debt amounting to 210,000,000,000 gold marks. It is from this figure that one must proceed in measuring the extent to which the world is burdened with the after-effects of the War, and not from the 36 or 38 milliards which represent the capital value of the German Reparation obligations. It is for these 210,000,000,000 that interest and amortisation have to be found, though at the time when these milliards were being expended they were so laid out that they do not bring in one pfennig of return. On the contrary, they were so expended as to destroy as much of the enemy's assets as possible—in other words, to do the utmost possible to reduce the productivity of the world economic system.

For even a world economic system, the payment of the interest on 210,000,000,000 gold marks is no trifle. Is it beginning to be evident why in all the counting-houses of the world the manufacturers are in a cold sweat over their calculations, even in countries which have no social welfare expenditure to add to the costs of production? Is it beginning to be evident why the landowners have hours of despair in which they consider in all seriousness whether it would not be better for them to give away their possessions, instead of putting into them year by year labours of which the yield hardly covers the bare cost? That some call despairingly for cartel agreements and others for protective duties, merely in order to provide a level of prices within which it will be possible to go on producing on endurable terms?

Shutting their eyes meanwhile to the fact that these remedies are all ineffective in the long run, that they can only be of momentary assistance, and that their very first repercussion will simply accentuate the evil which they are designed to remedy?

Alas! "In itself," industrial capital would still be perfectly well able to work at a profit so long as the tilled land continued to bring forth its fruits. What makes calculation impossible is the heavy burden of State expenditure laid on every single step of the process of production, not merely on the final finished product, but also on every ingredient of its cost, on the raw materials before they enter the factory, on the wages in the form of contributions, and so on. Everyone today grumbles at the State, makes Marxism or some other scapegoat responsible, declares that things would go better with a change of Government, or blames Reparations—rightly enough, only the amount is much too small to have been able to bring such trouble; very few give a thought to the fact that at the back of it all there is the interest on 210,000,000,000 gold marks to pay, interest that has at all costs to be extracted from the yield of world trade and industry, because the State, which has the power to command, commands it. The unearned income of these 210,000,000,000 weighs like a first mortgage on every single product that each one of us buys, because this unearned income is not called profit or return, but tax, and accordingly ranks before profit and return.

Not a few readers, perhaps, will have been objecting to all this: "What ever is the writer thinking of? The creditors who receive the interest or repayments for their loan property do not stick the bank-notes in their stockings. They pay them out straightway in one way or another and so return them to the market as purchasing power. That disposes of everything the writer has been saying. He would only be right if the creditors put the bank-notes repaid to them in the stove and burned them."

That is the same objection as the one that "the money remains in the country." A reader who has followed us attentively should not raise this objection. What does the purchasing power look like, this purchasing power into which the interest and amortisation of the loan service have been converted, after it has passed through the hands of the loan-holder and comes now back to the market?

We cannot but suspect, however, that this objection will be raised on many sides; let us, therefore, to make the matter clear, interpose the story of a hypothetical case. Anyone who has found what we have written to be correct may skip this story.

THE INSTRUCTIVE EXAMPLE OF THE INSANE REGENT

Let us imagine an isolated State with a population of, let us say, in order to think in round numbers, a hundred millions. This State has an internal debt of five milliard gold marks, and thus a debt per head of population of fifty marks. Such an indebtedness is quite low, the population will scarcely notice it. It corresponds roughly to the indebtedness of the United States before the War.

Now let us assume that a regent comes into power and manages, during his period of rule of only a few years, to increase this indebtedness twentyfold, or up to a round hundred milliard gold marks. The money is all to remain in the country, only it is not to be employed in the least degree productively. The regent has perhaps fallen a victim to a pathological building craze, but he builds such mad castles that his creations cannot even, like the Bavarian royal castles, be made remunerative by the tourist industry. It is not at all an easy matter to think out an absolutely unproductive employment for such large sums, but humanity has behaved in its time as unproductively as all this. The regent, perhaps, builds the maddest of architecture, but as soon as it is finished, he has it pulled down again. He finances all these buildings by internal loans. It is impossible to do it all at once, but the profits are mobilized again and again by successive loans. What will be the course of events? The "key industry" of building will earn large sums, money will roll on from it all over the country, and people will all be congratulating one another on the booming trade. Money will circulate faster and faster, prices begin to rise, and the masses begin to groan under the increasing cost of living. Again and again new issues at high rates of interest bring the temptation to fresh capital investment; the regent allows the contractors good profits, so that they always have money in hand for further purchases of loan stock, and, as a tremendous campaign is carried on to advertise each issue, the loans are always placed. Some people praise the regent as a genius, because, they say, he brings work into the country, and the figures show that the prosperity was never so great; others curse him because the masses are being squeezed to death by high prices. Now the regent dies, and the building comes at once to a stop. The successor to the throne proceeds energetically to clear off the loans. The burden of debt is now a thousand marks a head. On the one hand, for interest and amortisation of the State debts, issued at an average of five per cent, the country must find six to seven milliards, or more in a single year than the whole of the State debt before the unlucky regent began his reign. On the other hand, these six to seven milliards go annually into the pockets of the loan-holders in the form of interest and repayment. What happens to these milliards? A certain proportion of them goes back at once into the State exchequer in the form of taxation. Another portion, payable on the loan paper subscribed by small investors, now suffering from the high cost of living, is devoted with a sigh to consumption. They had been hoping that the stock certificates which they had saved up would assure them comfort in their old age, and see now with disappointment that the high cost of living is eating up all their interest. Much the largest part of the interest—namely, that part which goes to loan-holders who have grown rich through the building contracts and who do not need the income from their holdings for immediate consumption, does not come back into the commodity market. There is no inclination even to buy additional luxury articles, for there is not sufficient freedom from anxiety. The times have "changed." People no longer have the courage to cut a figure in the world, they no longer know on what scale one ought to save in order to safeguard one's children from every eventuality. That part of the interest and repayments is capitalized. Money in search of profitable investment piles up. The small business men, who have long been suffering from the high cost of living, the landowners, whose property no longer brings in any return, clutch greedily at first at the money, which they urgently need. The indebtedness grows. But soon the indebtedness reaches a level at which investment becomes risky for the creditors. It becomes more and more difficult to find safe opportunities for profitable investment. Every year the State debt service sets free six to seven milliards; where to place it? Meanwhile business gets worse and worse, State contracts have long since come to an end, there is no more work for the building workers; prices, however, do not as yet fall, for the population has got used to the increased prices; and the more turnover diminishes, the more the producers attach importance to keeping to the old price level and securing it by agreements. No alternative remains but to export the unutilizable capital.

In this hypothetical case there has not been a word about war, and not a word about Reparations. To give this picture a post-war colour, two assumptions only have been needed—that internal indebtedness is multiplied, and that the yield of the internal loans has been employed for unproductive purposes.

THE EFFECTS OF THE SERVICE OF AMERICAN LOANS IN PARTICULAR

Not a few German readers may, long ere this, have furiously cut us short with: "What's his game? The comparison is entirely misleading. The American debts are paid by the German taxpayer."

From the figures given, those readers might have seen already that that contention is inaccurate. The view is held, however, thanks to the newspapers, by very many German laymen; we will therefore go more closely into the facts.

As we have already seen, America's own debts amounted in 1929 to 16,900,000,000 dollars. Repayments had brought them down in 1930 to 16,700,000,000. Her arrangement, however, with her debtors had brought her claims against them down to only 12,000,000,000 dollars. Even this, as we saw, is only a nominal sum. The capital value of these 12,000,000,000, if we take an interest rate of four and a half per cent, is only 6,800,000,000 dollars (on the 1925 basis). America has herself, on the other hand, to pay fairly high interest rates on her war loans, so that it would correspond better with her own burden of interest to take an average rate of five per cent. At that rate the capital value of the American claims is actually no more than 5,900,000,000 dollars. Of the sum by which America's internal debts exceed this figure, no part is remitted by her creditors. To find the amount of this difference we must take the level of her debt in the same year, 1925. It stood then at 20,500,000,000. Thus America has herself to repay 14,600,000,000 dollars of her internal debts; what she receives from her debtors suffices only for the service of 5,900,000,000 of debt (on the 1925 basis).

It is necessary to be clear as to these circumstances to realize how severely, in spite of all repayments from her debtors, America is herself afflicted with the burden of war debts; and to realize also how unjust as well as undiplomatic it is for a certain section of the press continually to be calling America a Shylock. It is only too easy to understand if the American, who is thoroughly well aware of the burden of taxation in his own country, sees in the conferring of that sort of courtesy title nothing but evidence of Germany's ill will.

The picture becomes still clearer if instead of this bulk reckoning for the whole period of amortisation we look at the figures for a single year. The following figures show what would have been payable to America in 1931 if Mr. Hoover had not declared a year's moratorium. In 1931 America was due to receive:

	Million gold marks
Year's payments by the powers entitled to Reparations, being transfers from the German Reparation payments	980.0
From Germany direct (under the special agreement)	66.1
Total from Germany	1,046.1
From Great Britain, over and above her transfer of receipts from the German payments (amounting to 362,700,000 gold marks—the British liabilities to America for 1931 amounted to 669,700,000 gold marks)	307.0
Total	1,353.1

The preliminary estimates for the American federal budget for 1931 provided 619,000,000 dollars or 2,599,800,000 gold marks for the interest on public loans. Thus America had to pay 1,246,600,000 gold marks, or nearly half of the interest, herself.

The reader will, probably, at best note these figures with interest, and they will do nothing towards establishing our contention to his satisfaction. The evidence that counts is not what is to happen over a period of sixty-two years under the settlement plan (for it will not happen), but what has happened so far. What we want to do is to ascertain the course of events up to the present, and it is there, in what has happened, that we must seek for the causes.

Let us consider America once more, since that is the country that has the keys of the economic system of the world of today in its hands.

In the years 1919–30 America brought her internal debts down from 25,480,000,000 to 16,740,000,000 dollars. That is, to begin with, a mark of character. But what does it mean outside morality, in the purely economic field? In eleven years she liquidated 8,740,000,000 dollars, or 36,000,000,000 gold marks, which had been immobilized by the loans. That does not include the interest payments; including those the sum is substantially higher. For interest and amortisation America expended in the last six years:

1925–6	1,319,300,000 dollars
1926–7	1,306,600,000 dollars
1927–8	1,272,000,000 dollars
1928–9	1,227,900,000 dollars
1929–30	1,193,000,000 dollars
1930–1	1,254,300,000 dollars

We see that America has provided on an average a round milliard and a quarter of dollars annually of liquid capital for the loan-holders. In the first years after the War the sum was even higher than in the later years enumerated above, for America went very energetically to work with amortisation immediately after the War, and of course the interest service falls as amortisation proceeds. Multiplying this average sum by 11, we get the figure of 13,750,000,000 dollars, or 57,500,000,000 gold marks paid over by America to her creditors in the years 1919–30. Whence came these milliards, and where have they gone?

As for their source, we have just shown that even

under the Young Plan only half of the annual amount paid out came from foreign claims. But the full payments under the Dawes Plan only began with the year 1928. Before that the receipts from the foreign debtors were considerably smaller, and before 1924 the former Allies paid virtually nothing. It may be taken as a rough approximation that America provided some three quarters of these fifty-seven milliards of marks herself.

What became of them? Were they immediately devoted to consumption? That would have meant an increase in food prices and must have found expression in the American index number of the cost of living. A big increase in the prices of foodstuffs did, as a matter of fact, show itself in America in the first years after the War. The cost-of-living index number, which had climbed up to 187 by the end of the War, remained at that level during 1919 and then rose rapidly in 1920 to 219. Then, however, came the American crisis of 1921, with an unprecedented fall in food prices; the index number fell to 148 in June 1921, and in the years that followed it rose only slightly over 150. Thus, we must not look for the milliards in consumption.

Another index number, however, rose steadily and rapidly, the American index number of share prices. There began that unexampled rise in the level of share quotations on the American stock exchange that has often enough been described. The index number of Dow, Jones & Company takes the nominal value of twenty New York industrial shares as 100. These twenty industrial shares were quoted in 1923 at an average price of 94.6. In 1924 they rose to par, in 1925 to 134, in 1926 to 153, in 1927 to 180, in 1928 to 228, in January 1929 to 280, and in September 1929 to the record figure of 344. That meant that, in the eyes of the fortunate members of the public who had these shares in their safes, their value was three and a half times the value in 1924. But had the dividends also risen three and a half times? Only so would the rise in the shares have been justified. If one ventured to raise that question, one was informed that the times were past when the quotation depended on the yield; the quotation was determined by the "intrinsic value" of the paper. No one asked whether it was not really absurd to buy at a price representing twelve and more per cent a security that yielded only two per cent. The paper went on rising with unfailing regularity and yielded a price profit which amply brought in the twelve per cent per annum. The rise in quotations year by year was called "prosperity," and people were quite sure that it was going to go on for ever. In reality the rise in quotations was the quite simple result of the working of supply and demand. The fourfold rise in share prices was the expression of nothing more than the simple fact that the pressure on the share market of capital seeking investment was so great that it was no longer possible to buy more than two sevenths of what the same money would have bought in 1924. The simple laws of supply and demand are certainly familiar to every American, but in Wall Street at this period all the world forgot them. It is very easy now to describe the whole affair, after the event, as a psychosis. If one cannot explain something, one runs to the doctor, and the doctors run to Greek and Latin. To this day not a soul takes the trouble to think where the money can have come from to pay for the psychosis; what, in other words, was the source of the quadrupled purchasing power for stock-exchange securities. If one recalls the confusion that the French war indemnity brought after 1870 into German economic life, how apparent values then rose sky-high, until the crash came, there is no need to wonder if fifty-seven milliards produced many times as much confusion.

But is there not a tremendous error of the writer's to be seen here? The supply of the four milliards of gold marks to the German economic system ended with a crash because the payment was made only once. But the American interest payments are continuing; thus, the demand for securities must surely be continually being fed and the level of prices continually rise?

Anyone who raises that objection would only prove that in spite of all the writer's pains he has still failed to understand the difference between internal and external debts. The objection would be entirely justified if every bit of all the milliards came from abroad.

Since, however, the bulk of the milliards have to

be made available in the process of the internal debt service, the course of events was quite different. On the one hand the purchasing power for stock-exchange securities rose, on the other there set in the shifting of incomes which we have sufficiently clearly explained. The consuming power of the mass of the population fell. This latter process did not, it is true, become visible the moment it began, but only showed itself after it had been multiplied in the course of years.

In the first years it was masked by a very remarkable phenomenon, entirely peculiar to the American economic life of those years: by the so-called "financing of consumption." Suddenly people began in America to buy every pair of shoes on credit, and that without paying a single cent more than in the great stores next door that gave no credit. This "extension of credit trading" was regarded as a great step forward—why should not the retailer give credit just as the wholesaler does? Eager prophets of Americanism began at once to criticize Europe as reactionary because she did not there and then go over to the financing of consumption on the same scale. No one thought of asking how it was that this system had become economically possible and necessary—possible, so far as the seller was concerned, for him to give all this credit; necessary, so far as the buyer was concerned, for him to accept and be ready to pay for this system. Up to then the system of payment by instalments had been regarded as a particular affliction of the poor people, who, for lack of other sources of credit, had to pay the relatively high interest involved in instalment business. In America too the interest charged for this system of consumption by means of loans had always been extraordinarily high. The simple reason why all this business began nevertheless to be done was, so far as the credit-buyer was concerned, that he wanted to maintain his past standard of living, or even, in accordance with the general prosperity psychosis, to improve on it, while he had not the ready money with which to do so. On the side of the credit-giver the reason was that there was too much capital lying idle in the form of goods waiting for purchasers on a scale hitherto unusual. The capital invested in the way in loans to consumers has been estimated at eleven milliards of gold marks, and there are said to be five milliards still stuck fast in this business in the form of unpaid arrears. The figures are estimates which it is difficult to check; but they show that even before the outbreak of the crisis there was surplus capital competing for investment simultaneously with a fall in the purchasing power available for consumption—the symptoms of our crisis, want through superfluity. No one had at the time the faintest notion that the financing of consumption could be a harbinger of the crisis and the plainest first instalment of its symptoms. The new method of selling was cried up as a step forward, and no one even noticed the simple fact that providing credit for the turnover of goods is quite a different thing from providing credit for the consumption of goods.

The path of the financing of consumption was, however, only a small side-path taken by the capital set free through the debt service. We followed this side-path first only because it showed so prettily the setting in at the same time of a fall in the purchasing power of the mass of the population.

The main stream of the liberated money flowed into new investments. From the point of view of the receiver of the repayments, that is entirely a matter of course. The money came from loan property, until then it had been in permanent investment, and it was not desired to use that property, to become poorer than before; that would never have been permitted by the capitalistic conscience of the American. Accordingly, new opportunities of investment were sought.

"But if the money came out of investments and flowed into new investments, how could economic disturbances result?"

For the so-and-soth time we must correct this fallacy, this optical illusion. Though it is an illusion which deceived not only the American loan-holder but the whole capitalist world, and still deceives them day by day. The money came only nominally back from loans; in actual fact it had to be tapped from the economic system, and mainly from the American economic system itself.

Since the end of the War it has in this way been

uninterruptedly raining milliards in America, as it did in Germany after the Franco-German War, but with this tremendous difference, that these milliards had first been withdrawn mainly from America's own economic system. How can it be possible that the Americans have not yet grasped the importance of these facts? Well, to begin with, the milliards appeared as the direct continuation of the war profits. The first big reaction set in in 1921. The crisis in America at that time attracted comparatively little notice in Germany, all eyes being then fixed on Germany's western neighbour, and the situation within the country, in consequence of the slowly growing inflation, being not so bad. At that period America had about three and a half million workers unemployed. In 1922 there began the debt agreements with the Allies, the first payments began to arrive from the debtor countries, and from then on, the milliards pursued another course. The liberated capital began to be exported, in order to produce purchasing power abroad for American goods. Trade was thus revived, and the unemployed were absorbed once more by the labour market. The principal fields for loans were South America and California. South America especially was "glutted" with loans (cf. Report of the Federal Reserve Bank of New York on money-market conditions in 1930). Max Winkler calculates the present indebtedness of South America to the United States at twenty-two milliards of gold marks ("Investments of United States Capital in

Latin-America"). Before the War they can scarcely have been half as much. In California the milliards were employed in setting up the grain silos in which the surplus grain was conditioned that subsequently sent down the world market prices for wheat to a low level never before known.

The bulk of the milliards, however, wended their way to Europe. What did industrialized Europe do with the money? We have seen how the producers were in despair over their calculations, seeing no way of covering the interest on their capital on top of the burdens of taxation. Wages could not be reduced because the labour organizations were on the watch; the only remaining way out was to increase production in relation to overhead costs; in a word, rationalization. Then it was that all the political economists of Germany oracularly declared that nothing could help us but increased production. The poor manufacturers put faith in this and clutched the money offered in the capital market, although it was particularly dear, for no other reason than to carry through rationalization. So rationalization became possible and necessary—possible because the requisite capital was on offer in the capital market; necessary because it seemed to be the last means by which the producer could continue his production under the increased burden of taxation. The rationalization produced the spectacle of a transient, illusory trade boom, because it brought the capital borrowed for its work of alterations and extensions into consumption. The amount of capital introduced in this way into Germany in particular, in the form of long- or short-term loans, has often enough been calculated, lately in the report of the Basel Commission. The amount of capital invested in Germany in particular in the years 1924–8, and the form of investment, are described in the Inquiry of the Institut für Konjunkturforschung. In that Inquiry one may also read how much capital was invested uneconomically.

The total amount of the capital invested abroad by the United States is given by Ferdinand Fried, on the basis of details published by the American writer Max Winkler and by the *Index* (New York Trust Company), as 75,000,000,000 gold marks, against 20,000,000,000 before the War. That means an increase in the world's indebtedness to the United States since the War of 55,000,000,000 gold marks. That brings us very close to our 57,000,000,000. It can hardly be a mere chance that the figure given by this very well-informed author, on the basis of direct estimates of the capital sums sent abroad, agrees so closely with the figure which we have obtained from entirely different premisses.

TOWARDS A CONCLUSION

We recall that we found Dalberg's "fundamental impulse" inadequate. The shifting of a purchasing power of two milliards of gold marks from one State to another was not, in our view, a sufficient cause to account for the troubles of the world's trade and industry. This shifting would soon have corrected itself, and after a few disturbances due to the readjustment it would have left scarcely a trace. We asked where the amplifying energy could come from that would so multiply the shiftings of the two milliards as to make them responsible for losses of many times that amount in the world market.

Now we have discovered the amplifying energy. It was not provided by the shifting of the two milliards from country to country, but in what thereafter happened to the two milliards within the economic system of the receiving State, and also in the other shiftings, many times greater, that arose from the internal debt service. It is not enough to have regard only to the external debt service.

The internal debt service

1. releases the milliards which had been tied up in the war loans. These milliards seek reinvestment.

2. On the other hand, the foreign claims are far from sufficing to meet the internal debt service, and the bulk of the expenditure on this must be withdrawn from the country's trade and industry through the taxation of productive industry.

It is, in very truth, no new discovery that production has been burdened since the War with an extraordinary increase of taxation. German employers usually make the burdens of social welfare organization responsible for the burden of taxation and accordingly demand a retrenchment of the social organizations. America, however, has no social organization of the German type, and yet the taxation burdens of trade and industry have grown similarly.—Regarding the question from the point of view of capital, the productive capital of the world has to provide out of its yield not only the sums required for its own interest dues, but also the sums for the interest and amortisation payments on the dead capital of past war loans. It has thus to try to extract a higher income yield from the process of production. In other words, to try to increase the yield of production in relation to wages. The only way out seemed to be offered by rationalization.

In our criticism of the theories of the crisis we asked whether the economic leaders had completely taken leave of their intelligence when they cried out for increased production and urged on rationalization without asking whether the market for the increased production was assured—and now had the spectacle of only a fraction of the newly provided apparatus of production able to be used, and the outlay on the costly plant cursed as a blunder. We came to that question in consequence of a theory of the crisis which represented rationalization simply as a gift of technical progress—a progress which this time had unmasked to reveal itself as a devil after it had been worshipped throughout the nineteenth century as a god. Now we see that the unfortunate economic leaders had no choice. They all did their sums splendidly and seized the only chance of safety that was to be had. The devil was not in the rationalization, but in the debt service of the world indebtedness, pressing with one hand on the calculations in the form of taxation, and offering the surplus capital with the other hand for rationalization.

Since, in view of the burden of taxation, production can save the productive capital in no other way than by reducing the proportion of the wages costs in the final product (and if attacks on piece-work agreements are of no avail, rationalization does avail),

3. the share of the masses in the yield of the process of production grows steadily smaller. Consequently the consuming power of the masses in the markets of the world economic system is similarly reduced.

Thus the post-war economic system works under entirely different conditions from those of the pre-war system. It has to provide out of its yield not only the return on its own capital, but also the interest and amortisation of the dead debt capital. The only item that can be cut down is the cost of the proportion represented by the wages of labour. This is impossible by means of independent wage agreements—the organizations prevent it—and accordingly the aid of technical progress is sought and machinery is brought in to reduce as far as possible the labour element in the final product. Capital enough for this machinery is available through the liberation of capital by the repayment of loan stock. Since, however, the share distributed in wages is diminished, and since the incomes from wages are also reduced like other incomes by the tax administration, in order to provide the money for the debt service, the capacity for consumption has already fallen too low to be able to absorb the increase in production. So arises the paradox of the present crisis—want through superfluity.

All three of the factors enumerated must be taken together, or the chain of reasoning is left incomplete. Each one of the ideas brought forward has, of course, already been expressed in one quarter or another—in a matter like trade and industry in general, a matter on which everyone concerned in trade and industry has his own thoughts, there can naturally be no such thing as a new discovery. These ideas may therefore give to many readers the impression of being nothing more than a repetition of things long familiar. The essence of the argument lies in the interlocking of One, Two, and Three.

In all three factors, however, there lies, variously cloaked, one and the same economic force: the production and provision of the debt service for the unproductive war debts. In One are concealed the interest payments and capital repayments already made; in Two and Three is concealed the compulsion further to pay interest and amortisation of the loans still outstanding.

THE SEPARATOR OF PUBLIC INDEBTEDNESS

It needs a concrete illustration to make it clear how the public debt service can work both ways, reducing incomes on one hand and increasing them and consequently forming capital on the other. How can such contradictory effects proceed from one and the same cause? Is it not a defiance of the simplest laws of logic? Many critics will probably say: "The writer has thought out a scapegoat for all the trouble—the public debt service (perhaps he is feeling the pinch of taxation himself). He loads up this scapegoat with every burden that shows itself—decline in purchasing power, surplus of capital, excessive production, falling sales. He carries through his thesis with plenty of dialectics, makes a good show with his scapegoat; but all this has nothing to do with ascertaining the true facts."

We shall therefore make this paradox clearer by one more special illustration—this paradox that apparently contradictory effects are being produced by one and the same cause, a paradox that is, in fact, the peculiar feature of the present crisis. If one pours into the bowl of a separator a quantity of milk and sets the separator in rotation, no change whatever is produced in the total quantity of the contents of the bowl. Total weight, total volume of the fatty and defatted portions together remain absolutely the same, so long as nothing is splashed over the top. Yet something quite different is made of the milk: it is divided into full cream and skim milk. The public debt service is nothing but a rotation of the national income. The total amount of the national income remains unaltered, but the private incomes are divided into full cream and skim milk. The full-cream incomes collect around the rim; out of income there has come, simply through the rotation, newly produced capital, which demands investment and ultimately goes out of the country. The milk that remains grows thinner and thinner the longer the rotation continues, losing more and more of its content—its purchasing power. And the economic gulf grows wider and wider, the middling incomes are steadily swept away.

Can the critics get rid of the separator by declaring that an increase of the full cream and a simultaneous increase of the skim milk are two contradictory effects and therefore cannot be produced by the same cause?

THE TEST FROM A PARTICULAR CASE

We began our demonstration with the American economic system. We are curious to see how the argument set forth tallies with the economic situation in the other principal creditor countries. Can there be anything more radically different than the economic fate of Britain and France in recent years? Wealthy Britain involved today in a crisis; France, once regarded as so weak, with her currency apparently falling to nothing, suddenly in possession of the second largest gold reserve in the world—how can these two developments be made intelligible?

We recall that Great Britain's burden of debt has also been multiplied several times over by the War.

Her external indebtedness rose to 1,080,000,000 pounds in 1929; the interest and amortisation of the external debts swallowed up 35,000,000 pounds. This amount, however, is more than covered by incomings from credits abroad. At this rate British trade and industry should be doing very well, if the internal debts may be left out of account as irrelevant to the general condition of the country's economic system, because "the money remains in the country." In actual fact, British trade and industry are in such convulsions as have only been witnessed in the darkest moments of the country's history. Consider the internal debt; it is six and a half times the amount of the external. The internal debt service (interest and amortisation) swallowed up 319,000,000 pounds in 1925–6, 340,000,000 pounds in 1929—41.1 per cent and 43.2 per cent of the budget. It is true that a substantial part of this is covered by receipts from abroad, and this part would be still larger if Britain's claims were not in a bad way in many parts of the world. In any case, the British people has itself to provide annually through taxation for its internal debt service over 150,000,000 pounds, or three milliard gold marks—one and a half times the German Reparation payments. Consequently, when the Germans complain of the intolerable burden of Reparations, people regularly point in Britain to their own much heavier burdens and are inclined to take the German complaints as evidence of lack of goodwill. A people of such political intelligence should know better, for the effect of the taxation on the general *taxable capacity* is, obviously, quite different if the money remains within the country. On the other hand, the German habit of regarding the internal debt service as a sort of mere question of circulation is also erroneous. What happens to the milliards of the internal debt service?

Mr. Philips Price has estimated the British investments abroad before the War at 85,000,000,000 gold marks and at present at 124,000,000,000. That makes an increase of 39,000,000,000 since the end of the War. We mentioned just now that the British people has to provide annually for its internal debt service over 3,000,000,000 gold marks. Multiply these three milliards by 13, the number of years since the end of the War, and we arrive at the figure of 39,000,000,-000. Most of this capital may remain within the economic system of the Empire, but, for all that, it makes a great difference whether the amount itself or merely the interest on it circulates in the circulatory system of the mother country's consumption. In actual fact, the export of the additional capital provided by the debt makes the British capitalist steadily richer, but the country steadily poorer.

France seems to be dancing entirely out of time. Let the explanation of the situation of the French economic system be our test from a particular case. What has not been offered by way of explanation of the French "island" in the ocean of unemployment! Since 1930 France has suddenly been proclaimed as the French economic miracle. One can only wonder that the economic writers are not ashamed to type the phrase. How long is it since the French franc had fallen on its nose and its revalorization had reached the limits of the possible—and every newspaper was writing that the French had no gift of large initiative and were deficient in the modern economic spirit? There has been less talk of the French economic miracle since the first signs of unemployment began to show themselves in France. But what great achievement have the French to their credit, how have they managed to get the gold piling up every week in the vaults of their Bank to a new record level? Reply—they have done nothing. Above all, they have not rationalized, have not checkmated their consumers. Why have they not done so? Have they been restrained by economic insight, by the instinct of the ant as it strokes the aphis—to "milk" it, not to kill it? That is unlikely, for the French capitalist is no less egotistical than the Anglo-Saxon. The riddle is solved when one considers France's debts. At the end of the War she owed enormous sums to America and Britain. The debts were in foreign currency, and as the franc fell, France's position became very serious. The fall in the currency was going on at the time of the debt negotiations, and the French made very skilful diplomatic use of it; they succeeded in getting considerable proportions of the debts remitted. The result is that France's liabilities to her foreign creditors are exceeded by her share in German Reparations by 388,000,000 gold marks. And her internal debt situation is incomparably better than that of either of the two great Anglo-Saxon countries. In 1925 her internal debt service required 13,075,000,000 francs (2,200,000,000 gold marks); in 1928, 16,900,000,000 francs (2,900,000,000 gold marks). There is material for a crisis here too, but we need not imagine that the French figure of unemployment will advance with giant strides like those of Germany and Britain. For the French debt separator is working at only one fifth of full speed.

This fortunate economic situation is thus not the result of special economic acumen. It has, indeed, been presented to this lucky country actually against its will. Had Monsieur Poincaré attained the goal which he made such efforts to reach, and stabilized the franc at par, and had France accordingly to bear today five times her existing internal debt, her position would probably be worse than Britain's. The French *rentier,* when he looks at his Bank of France notes and grieves because they buy only one fifth as much now, does not know what he is complaining about.

Chapter Five

SUMMING UP

When America began to get in the money that she had lent to the former Allies, her action was sharply criticized on moral grounds. That never made much impression on the Americans. They took up the simple standpoint that "We lent the money." Mr. Mellon himself referred to the moral aspect of the matter: "I doubt whether European nations dislike us as much as some people tell us they do. But I know this, that if they do, the cancellation of that part of their debts which has not already been cancelled will not of itself change their dislike into affection. Neither in international relations any more than in private life is affection a purchasable commodity, while my observation and reading of history lead me to conclude that a nation is hardly likely to deserve and maintain the respect of other nations by sacrificing its own just claims."

The argument was next shifted to purely economic grounds, and the Reparation payments were represented as harmful to world trade, inasmuch as they weakened an important customer, Germany, and reduced her capacity to buy in the world market. One may energetically advance this argument, but, after all, it cannot be anything but a confirmation to the victor States of their policy. If Germany is absent from the world market today as consumer, she will be absent tomorrow as producer, for, of course, she has no raw materials. And however eloquently one's figures may demonstrate that the Young Plan is economically irrational, because it is devised to make the gold flow uphill, those who stand on the hill-tops will reply that the plan is functioning admirably, and that if it had not been there, it would have been necessary to invent it.

The argument of this book has followed quite a different line. We have not considered the debt payments left behind it by the War from the point of view of Germany or of any individual State, but from the point of view of the productive capital of the world economic system (not from that of demand in the world market). We chose this point of departure because all values in the world are the product solely of the collaboration of labour and capital.

Regarded from the point of view of world trade and industry, the war debts are seen to be a liability which has no corresponding asset. This liability, after taking account of all remissions and agreements for amortisation, we have calculated at a round 210,000,000,000 gold marks. These 210,000,000,000 demand their interest and amortisation although no productive asset in the shape of any capital expenditure or the like can be put over against them. On the contrary, they were subscribed expressly in the service of the destruction of assets. If such items stood in the accounts of any private business, they would long ago have had to be written off or the business would have gone under. Had the World War been waged by a private capitalist, or by two—and the times are not so long past when *condottieri* carried on wars on their own account—both would long ago have gone bankrupt. Since, however, the prestige of the victor States is bound up with these liabilities, they are retained in full and carried forward as though they represented living capital, no matter how much that business enterprise, World Trade, suffers.

Productive capital is struggling desperately against this liability and has no other resource than to try to provide out of its own yield the income needed to pay the interest and amortisation on it, by carrying to the utmost possible limit the technical cheapening of production (rationalization).

Since the capital liability of the war loans is balanced by no real asset, it must (regarded from the point of view of productive capital) be set down as extra capital. The world's economic system is struggling instinctively—so surely as every crisis is an illness of which the purpose is to aid recovery—to eliminate the extra capital. For no undertaking is sound unless the capital standing in its books bears a healthy relationship to the productivity of the undertaking. This simple rule is familiar to every company board, and it should not be so difficult to bring it into application for world trade. It is good evidence of the healthy constitution of the world's economic system that it has already brought down the dead weight of war debts from the original thousand milliards of gold marks to two hundred and ten milliards. But now it looks as if world trade is intended to be left saddled with this remainder.

For all that, the world's economic system will have to go further so surely as every fresh day brings its day's work. And if that liability is maintained by main force for political reasons, there remains no other course open to the economic system than for the other capital, the productive capital, to be reduced. For a writing off there has to be, so much is certain, and in the last resort it makes no difference to the economic system, since it must live, at what point it writes down its capital. If the unproductive loan capital is held on to, the productive capital will dwindle away. For humanity that carries the painful corollary that there will then be a diminution of production itself and a shrinkage of trade.

One may put it that the world is suffering from its books. That sounds like an evil dream, scarcely credible in an age so exclusively concerned with "reality." But so it has always been in history—reality has had to play second fiddle to the imagination. How much blood was shed, how much wealth destroyed, over the question whether the Host contained the Body of the Lord in actual fact or only symbolically! Later generations may find the present crisis just as incredible as that, though the books from which we are suffering are of the very opposite sort to those of the conflicting confessional catechisms. The figures in our ledgers seem to us a mere reflection of reality; never, one might suppose, could they have any force over against "reality itself." And yet every trader knows how crucial a difference it makes to the progress of his business on which side his books balance.

The world is suffering from the figures which stand in its books. Since the War it has been suffering from the extra capital of the war debts, suffering from capital inflation.[1] The crisis itself is to be understood as a process of capital deflation, of the elimination of surplus capital. This process will be insidious and cruel if world trade is left to itself as hitherto. It will result in the dwindling away of production and finally in the ruin of the firm called "World Trade" if the dead hand of the debt liability is given precedence over the living capital. It can be cut short and turned into a new revival of trade, never by leaving world trade to look after itself and merely keeping a look-out for symptoms of revival, only by energetically writing off in the proper quarter.

[1] We use the word "capital" here in its popular sense, as a sum of money that brings in interest. That this capital is not capital in the economic sense is the whole thesis of this book. The words "credit inflation" have a special current meaning; they are used for an expansion of short-term credit owing to relatively low discount rates and so on. The correct phrase to use above would be "inflation of long-term loan credit."

CONFIRMATION

A physical theory—the theory, for instance, of light—is correct when is gives as comprehensive an explanation as possible of the various phenomena of the physics of light. The confirmation of our theory lies in the fact that it explains many phenomena which are peculiar to this crisis and distinguish it from others.

1. To begin with, it becomes intelligible why this crisis is manifesting itself everywhere in the impossibility of balancing budgets. Everywhere the treasury departments and the ministers of finance are in desperation. Past crises have not worked out in this way. Their pressure rested mainly on the shoulders of the producers, while the State officials looked on from their offices in bureaucratic imperturbability. There might be a fall in taxation revenue, but within incomparably narrower limits. Cause: there was not the present pressure of the public debt service on the budget.

2. The special peculiarity of the present crisis we found in Chapter ii to be: want through superfluity. This did not manifest itself in the present form in earlier crises. Superfluity might present itself in another way in crises of production, at the point where sales had come to a stop—for instance, among industrial products. This surplus was taken up so soon as a surplus was produced at another point—for instance, through a good harvest. Then the farmers

were able to buy up the excess production of the manufacturers, and equilibrium was gradually restored. In the present crisis want exists alongside superfluity simultaneously in the most varied quarters—superfluity of foodstuffs while millions of unemployed are hungry and the yet more numerous millions of the pinched middle classes cut down their purchases; surplus of tonnage with shortage of freights; surplus of unemployed capital and yet long-term credits not to be had. The law of the equilibrium of supply and demand seems to have been abrogated. It seems a hopeless problem ever to work off surplus and want against each other, since both exist simultaneously at various points and both go on increasing. We have shown what it is that produces this simultaneous increase in opposite directions—the separator of the debt service.

3. The secret of excessive rationalization is discovered. This rationalization no longer takes on the semblance of the product of a technical inventiveness suddenly turned to mania—that inventiveness which up to now all liberal economists had worshipped as the bringer of progress, now revealed as the bringer of disaster. Inventions are made theoretically when they occur to the inventive spirit; they are realized in practice when they seem to trade and industry to be capable of yielding a profit. That has been precisely the career of rationalization: Taylor had published his system long before the War. All economic things come from economic reasons. We have

shown how it was that rationalization became economically possible and necessary. At the same time we found that the crisis is only superficially a "crisis of rationalization." The precipitate rationalization was itself a consequence of the industrial difficulties, not their cause. Had the calculations been free of the pressure of the taxation arising from the war indebtedness, and had the extra capital, on the other hand, not been available for the rationalization, the rationalization would have proceeded organically—that is, in accordance with the growth of capital formation out of the yield of productive capital—and would never have produced these devastating results.

This answers at the same time those who might object that rationalization would have come in any case, war debts or none. "Certainly so," these objectors will add; "without the War there would have been no piling up of war debts, and rationalization would have been proceeded with even earlier. In any case we should have had rationalization just as it has come, for it lay in the path of development, and it would have brought with it the rationalization crisis. The difference in economic development with and without the War cannot be so very great."—To that one must reply: It is one of the articles of faith of the capitalist system that the formation of new capital has to come from the surpluses that are tapped from the yield of production. That process automatically sets due limits to the formation of new capital and to new capital outlay. We have seen how many milliards the American State alone handled in the debt service, drawing them out of the national economic system in the form of taxes and duties and distributing them as interest and amortisation. Will anyone suggest that without the service of the war indebtedness the same milliards would have been diverted from the yield of production and accumulated by simply retaining them? That would never have happened, for it would never have been possible. It is generally a little dangerous to argue with "if" and "suppose," but this is demonstrable. For the pressure which the State is exerting today in every country, debtor and creditor countries alike, by means of taxation, could never have been applied by private capital, however rigidly cartellized. The consumers would not have stood it. Only the State can make people so tighten their belts. In consequence of the economic system on which the War was carried on, the State has taken over in the victor countries the function of capital formation and is carrying it on with the blind conscientiousness of a State on a scale which these creditors could never have approached without the State. The result has been to throw the formation of new capital, the new capital outlay, and so the whole capitalist machinery out of balance. Once more it is a question of relative magnitudes. Without the War, rationalization would certainly still have come, but it would have presented a very different appearance. It would not have been built, so to speak, in a day, so much so that the branches of industry affected actually had to restrict production the moment they were ready to begin producing on the grand scale. It would have come organically and would have grown step by step with the growing consumption. Never would it have been inaugurated as a sort of desperate remedy, as the last hope of escaping from a monstrous pressure of taxation; never would calculations have been made simply as calculations of production; they would have been made at the same time as sales calculations. So far as Germany herself is concerned, the rationalization of industry as a thing apart would never have been pushed on, in the desperate hope that the Reparation milliards might be got from the yield of increased exports; rationalization would have developed entirely of its own accord, and by parallel steps in industry and agriculture. All these are no arbitrary assumptions; sensitive self-regulation of this sort is second nature with capitalist trade and industry.

4. The regional differences in the extent of the crisis are explained. No other theory has succeeded in explaining these differences from one single principle. On the contrary, these differences have actually been made use of negatively as proof that there is no connexion between the burden of Reparations and the crisis. How, it has been argued, can the crisis be due to the Reparation payments when the creditor countries are just as hard hit by it as the debtor country, Germany? This argument belongs to the regular

stock of the liberal and majority Socialist politician. It does, indeed, look clinching—so long as one has regard only to external war indebtedness. That certainly shows no correspondence whatever with intensity of crisis. If, however, one brings into consideration, as we have done, the internal indebtedness as well as the external, one may lay down the proposition as very close to the truth that: a country has to suffer under the crisis the more acutely the more heavily it is burdened with debt arising out of the War, whether it be the direct burden of internal indebtedness or the indirect burden of treaty-imposed transfer liabilities as in Germany. To have to produce interest for unproductive capital drains away the substance of any country's trade and industry, and accordingly it makes no difference whether the country was a victor in the War or a defeated country. Now it is clear why rich America is competing with poor Germany in number of unemployed, and why France is in a position to pull the pound off its gold saddle and to draw in American gold, although the franc never has had and never will have anything like the importance in the world's commerce of the pound and the dollar.

5. We understand now why Mr. Hoover's moratorium year has not revived trade as was expected. It was wrong to set exaggerated expectations on the year's moratorium, and it is a still greater wrong to say that Hoover is "done for" because undue expectations remained unfulfilled. The truth is that the post-

ponement of payment has been very far from ineffectual: the fact that the mark is still on a gold basis is entirely due to Mr. Hoover's intervention. But nobody thinks of that, for people had promised themselves quite different results. The blame for the fact that these much wider hopes were not realized is generally thrown on French policy, which postponed the coming into force of the Hoover plan so long as to rob it of much of its psychological effect. That may serve to account for the acute crisis in the German money market in July. But the events that followed, the fall in sterling, the raising of the discount rate in the gold-holding countries in spite of falling trade, and so on, are not to be explained simply by "psychological factors." The rudest of hard facts are at work there, uninfluenced in the slightest in their force or duration by Mr. Hoover's action. The whole system has remained unaltered, unaffected by any Hoover plan. A whole year's grace still gets a day less with every day that passes, as every soldier knows from his service with the colours. How should any further effect come of the plan if there was no immediate effect? The whole Hoover year was simply a plaster, and not only that, but one that grew smaller every day by 1/365th. At the critical moment a plaster may save a life. That does not alter the fact that it is only a plaster, and when it has been applied, a start still has to be made with the actual treatment. Mr. Hoover contented himself with the plaster because he had not the courage for a thoroughgoing medical treatment and, above all, because he had no knowledge of the fundamental cause. From our whole argument it can be seen clearly that, for instance, a postponement merely of the external payment obligations could not in the least alter the fact that the State budgets were in difficulties everywhere; and was not it precisely at that point that the British crisis set in? The Hoover year's moratorium has effected what in the nature of things it was possible for a mere postponement of payment merely of the external debts merely for one year to effect. Let those who are disappointed lay the blame on their own excessive expectations.

OBJECTIONS

1. It might be objected that: "The war indebtedness has been in existence since the War began, or, if one wants to consider it in relation to a warless economic system, since 1918; the world crisis dates from 1929. How can the cause for an event be assigned to a condition which had already been in existence for ten years?"

Is it really necessary once more to mention, in order to meet that objection, all the buffers that received and mitigated the impact of the financial effects of the public debt service up to 1929? Must we recall how in the early years after the War the repayments of the international debt service came in only sparingly, and how the whole system of the international plans of amortisation only came into force, with the full annual payments, precisely in 1928–9?

In the first years after the War, America effected her amortisation almost entirely out of her own internal resources, while Europe had embarked on the policy of sanctions; and promptly America produced her crisis, the crisis of 1921, which travelled from America to Europe. America was then the country of origin of the crisis—can there be a neater confirmation of our theory? Then it was that locomotives were stoked for the first time with wheat, and then that the phrase "buyers' strike" was coined. In those years the world was still too much under the influence of the immediate consequences of the War; many people ascribed the crisis to the elimination of Russia under her Bolshevik régime. In any case, people did not rack their brains very much to discover causes, for the consequences of the War, then still a recent thing, offered troubles enough to serve as causes, currency troubles above all. The whole crisis had, indeed, developed in the background of war conditions that had not yet been got rid of, and not, like the present crisis, in contrast to a prosperity that had been supposed to be stable. Then there came into use the word "reconstruction." And reconstruction went on, while America hit on the idea of systematically exporting capital in order so to create purchasing power for her customers. Of all possible results of this, no one imagined that ten years later everything would be as before, only with all the havoc of the crisis ten times worse.

The whole of the middle years of the past decade

were characterized in America by continual export of capital. It was believed that in this mechanism of capital export and double profit from the debtor—through the interest that he paid and through the goods that he was in a position to buy in consequence of the capital lent—there had been discovered the recipe for ever-increasing prosperity. Whether it could be possible for this system of over-capitalization to go on for ever, no one troubled to inquire.

We described the internal aspects of these buffers—stock-exchange speculation, financing of consumption. An important point is that the much-discussed rationalization was simply a term in this series. For, regarded from the point of view of capital, the rationalization was this same prosperity-promising system of capital outlay. The money came out of investment, in the form of State paper, and was seeking reinvestment. The rationalization was, so to speak, the last buffer. It offered good interest to the creditor, and if the debtor sighed as he paid, his conscience was clear, for the multiplication of production was to bring it all in again. At the same time the rationalization work set the borrowed money in circulation, so that the fall in the consuming power of the masses did not yet show itself. When after that the excess production due to rationalization proved unsalable, there was no further buffer left. Then at last it became mercilessly clear what the world had been doing for over a decade.

2. Another objection raised is: "It is simply not

true that the war loans are 'dead.' The writer seems to believe that they are all in the hands of the shareholding class, who have them lying in their safes. In reality the loans were long ago mobilized; most of them are in the hands of the banks, which have based further credits on them"—and so on.

This is to apply the word "dead" in a different sense. We call the war debts a dead burden on world trade, but not in the sense in which one speaks of dead or "fallow" capital, as though they were actually existing capital that had been left idle and brought in no interest. What has happened is just the opposite: the capital has no actual existence, but does bring in interest. The war loans are a dead burden in the economic sense: there is no tangible asset corresponding to them in the realm of the process of production.

What in this objection is called "mobilizing" is the use as a basis of credit of the future interest receipts, and this does nothing whatever to alter the fact that these interest receipts do not come from the application of the loan moneys, but from other sources.

3. Other objections go deeper. Our whole conception is based on the two ideas of world trade and productivity, and objections could be hitched on to either. It might be said that "the writer throws open the ledger of the world economic system—but this system has no existence whatever. When we come to the accounts, the only things that really exist are the national economic systems, which stand in relation to

one another no differently from private business people. The world economic system has no business individuality; it is a convenient phrase invented by the experts and nothing more. The thesis that the writer brings forward is a pretty fancy, but unfortunately there is no real 'asset' corresponding to it."

There is this to be said in reply to that: If the world goes on as it has done, things will soon have gone so far that that objection will be justified. At present the world economic system has a real existence, even though it is steadily fading away. It is true that every State has been guided purely by its own economic egoism; all of them have calculated in the exact spirit of that objection. It was precisely the fact that this calculation proved mistaken that surprised all the world. Every State was out simply to get as much as possible for itself out of the "liquidation of the war"; no State thought of using any part of the product of liquidation to strengthen its holdings in the weakened joint firm of World Trade (which could have been done by cancelling debts, as Britain proposed). And so the stage was arrived at in which the assets entered in the books of the creditor States reached such figures as had never been known before, and yet their economic turnover fell and their balances grew worse month by month. How is that possible? It is only conceivable when one realizes that the books of the national economic systems are not the final books, but all these entries appear again in the accounts of world trade. Those accounts are not set down in writing, but there is not a moment's mystery or doubt about what would appear in them. If one imagines this world trade account to be made up and balanced, then all the riddles of the crisis solve themselves.

It is not even true that what comes into one national economic system comes out of the rest, and nothing else happens. Every shifting of assets from one nation to another affects also in some measure the holding of the partner in question in the jointly conducted firm of World Trade, and so affects the property and the productivity of that firm.

Anyone who is unprepared to believe this—that over and above the national economic systems there is the world economic system, an undertaking with its own productivity, on the earning capacity and the turnover of which the productivity of the national systems depends—will find the proof of the fact precisely in the surprise of this world crisis. For *the fact that it was not possible to localize this crisis on the defeated countries is only comprehensible on the assumption that there is a separate productivity of the world economic system,* over and above the national systems and determining their fate.

To make this clear from the crudest of illustrations, let us suppose that the Germans had grown tired of their federal system and, in a revived spirit of particularism, decided to leave each province to look after its own "economic area," and to return tomorrow to the pre-1866 status, thus separating into a multiplicity of independent States. Everyone can feel instinctively how much economic productivity would be destroyed by that step. The world is now very busily occupied in destroying economic productivity in precisely the same way. Not by tariff walls—these, as we saw, are effects and therefore secondary phenomena. The process of partition is much more direct. We know the difficulties into which the budgets actually of the rich creditor States have got in consequence of the burdens of the debt service. These difficulties are compelling every State to think all the time only of immediate incomings; that is, to get as much as possible out of the world economic system, not to put anything into it.

The whole of the development of the last hundred and fifty years has been characterized by the building up of greater and greater economic units. This has generally been attributed to national feeling—and in the realm of the emotional that attribution is certainly right. But in earlier times there were just the same communities of speech and of physiological origin; why did they not lead earlier to the formation of these unities? Those smaller States and economic groups, on the contrary, developed quite other loyalties, which strike us now as provincial or even parochial. And to this day the boys of Garmisch fight the boys of Partenkirchen, although they meet at the same station to receive the bringer of their bread, the foreigner. The regional loyalty has its field of effectiveness, but is not a sufficient explanation. What enabled the sense of a greater unit to bring that unit into effective existence was a new element—the realization that the formation of greater units opened up opportunities for productivity on a new scale. The dawning of that realization—one is reminded of Friedrich List—virtually coincided with the introduction of railways.

The history of the nineteenth century is characterized by the opening up of new stages of productivity through the formation of new economic units. Liberal economic science integrated that process in its imagination before the War, and with such precipitancy that it thought that the end of all wars had come.

If the creditor States further continue their present policy at the expense of world trade, we are likely to find ourselves at the great turning-point away from these formations of larger unities. But in that case we shall have also to realize that this return to the past means a rapid decline in world productivity and therewith in the standard of living.

The return to the past is already being recommended as a medicine. For it is a mysterious irony of our existence that maladies reinforce themselves and grow chronic by taking on the semblance of therapy and forming a habit. The future inebriate is positive that his flask of burgundy is just the thing that does him good, the incipient arteriosclerotic swears by his beefsteak, the neurotic by his coffee—until one day the collapse comes and the doctor urges a break with the habit. Will the world economic system of today and those who are responsible for it find the energy for a break? As yet (and who knows whether it is not the last chance?) we see the very opposite, as yet we see the very course recommended as a cure that accentuates the evil. Because world trade grows daily less in volume, are we to infer that the right course and actually the cure is for the nations to withdraw from it altogether and retire each into its own "self-sufficient" economic system? The recipe seems amazingly simple: if there is no longer a world economic system, there can no longer be a world economic crisis.

Undoubtedly all things are possible. We can, after all, begin the day with roasted flour soup, for the Germans lived before the Turks brought coffee to Vienna. Only it must be realized that in that case everything would be sacrificed that had been so many decades in the achieving through the development of higher economic units. After all, world trade has not developed as a sort of luxury article or out of love for sea trips; it came into existence because it was fruitful, because it was the cheapest way of satisfying certain needs. Undoubtedly Germany can in theory return to the pre-1866 status. But if it is patent at once to everybody that that would mean falling back to a lower level of productivity, would mean the smashing of a unit of which the formation was a great historic event, why should it be any different when it is the world economic system that is being smashed in order to fall back to a multiplicity of "self-sufficient" economic areas?

4. Amid all this talk of productivity one must not lose sight of the objection that not a few readers have probably been making in their minds for a long time past: "The writer's argument is based on the hypothesis that war expenditure is unproductive expenditure. Is that true of all war expenditure and of all wars? Or only for a part of the expenditure and only for the last war? Undoubtedly there have been wars which surely were economically productive. The war of 1870 brought Germany an enormous increase in her productivity. Must one describe the expenditure on it as unproductive? There is no need to go so far as the old philosopher who called war the father of all things, and consequently, one must infer, of productivity in particular, or as Darwin, who attributed to the struggle for existence the creative faculty of producing new species. There is, in any case, surely no denying that war has its creative faculties. But where is the line to be drawn?"

At the risk of calling down on ourselves the wrath of all the war enthusiasts—it is *precisely* in the economic field that virtually all war expenditure is unproductive. It is just this that gives the officer his magnificence, that makes the attraction of a soldier's life in war, giving him his sporting chance of living like a lord: the whole principle is to spend the money and damn the consequences. Let the civilians pay, let peace time pay, let the beaten enemy pay—war only does the spending. Mars is reckless with his money; hence his attraction for Venus. All that is productive in the sense of bringing in a direct economic return is the plant set up for war purposes, in so far as the war does not itself wear it out; in the last war, for instance, nitrogen-factories above all, convertible munition-factories, buildings of any sort which survive the War, good bridges, and so on. All other war expenditure is in itself unproductive, it can only become productive indirectly through the consequences of the war, in so far as these may be productive.

The deficiency of war in direct productivity probably explains the lack of any great Jewish record in war; the history of the Jews seems to contain no record of any great warlike initiative—a very surprising thing in view of the great vitality of the race. It can be no mere chance that Jesus ben Sira gave the warning that "War must be waged with prudence."

Indirectly war may be of the greatest productivity in the economic life of the belligerent country, if it gets rid of unhealthy conditions and sets up "healthy" (which, of course, means productive) conditions in their place. The wars of national union offer examples enough. Productivity only begins, however, after the war, with the new economic conditions which it has produced: first of all there is always plenty for the industries of peace to do to make good the damage of war. In order to enjoy the indirect productive effects of a war it is by no means absolutely necessary for the country concerned to be the victor on the battle-field.

The history of fortunate Italy offers examples enough of the way in which a country may be beaten in the field and yet be benefited by a war. For the real productivity secured through a war is not secured in any way at the cost of the enemy. The productive effect of the war of 1870 for Germany did not depend in the slightest on the milliards which France had to pay—these did almost as much harm as good; and they were, after all, not much more than the refunding of the actual costs incurred. The productive effect of that war depended on the new advance in productivity begun through Germany's union into a single economic body.

Entirely distinct from that is the other indirect productivity of a war, the productivity secured at the expense of the vanquished by making him pay the whole costs of the enterprise. The hope of productivity of this sort was responsible in the last war for the reckless piling up of debts on both sides.—But was not that hope entirely justified, was it not the expression of confidence in victory, which, after all, every belligerent is perfectly entitled to have?

Undoubtedly. Only, there is a fixed limit to this hope in the capacity of the adversary to pay. It is, of course, not genuine productivity, it is not the opening of a new advance in productivity, it is only a confiscation at the cost of the vanquished. And here we come back to what we have said above in regard to orders of magnitude. The question cannot be decided on any question of principle, but only from the point of view of magnitude. The mistake that was made was that the War went on too long. The vanquished can pay the cost of a short and sharp war; but after a certain point the war will go on at the expense of the substance of both parties. Then the attempt to force the vanquished to pay not only permanently diminishes the substance of the vanquished (which is just what the victor would want), but also destroys the level of productivity on which victor and vanquished alike stand. Then the peace does not pay for the war, but the war continues its destructive work under the name of peace.

Be it not objected that this is a transparent piece of special pleading for the vanquished and a pushing of the German case—the thing we set out to avoid. The evidence of the accuracy of what has been said is provided by the case of Russia. Russia was not the enemy of the Allies, only their debtor. Her withdrawal from the old form of trading on the basis of capitalist credits not only brought the creditor States the loss of all that they had advanced, but also enormously reduced the productivity of their trade and industry, so far as these depended on the Russian market. The creditor States are doing their best to add to this a like reduction of the productivity of their trade and industry so far as they depend on the German market.

That exhausts the productivity of war; it has no other. What we have called "indirect" productivity is ample to justify the title of war to the fatherhood of some immense things. Its productivity for the private capitalist in war industries (army contractors and financiers) is no reinforcement of the productivity of the national economic system. These profits are shiftings of assets *within* the national economic system, at the cost of the rest of the community. So surely as the basis of the greatest fortunes was laid during the War, so surely was it laid at the expense of the community. The Stinnes fortune, which began to be formed during the War and reached its top point during the inflation period, was built up entirely at the cost of the community, for the German national income did not become a pfennig greater during that period.

We find, therefore, that the direct productivity of the last war is confined to the development of the nitrogen industry and the strengthening of certain other industries concerned with the war, particularly the chemical industry, the aviation industry, the production of substitute raw materials, and so on. All other expenditure was unproductive in its direct effects. Indirectly the war opened the way to no advance in productivity; on the contrary, through partitions and uneconomic demarcations of territory the pre-war level of productivity was largely destroyed. Probably the only indirect service to productivity was the creation of Czechoslovakia. The effort to give the War an illusory productivity "at the cost of the others" is only too intelligible under the promptings of the instincts of the victor, but, in consequence of the magnitude of the cost of the War, it is leading to a destruction of the economic unity formed by the world's economic system, and so to the reduction of the level of productivity of which that economic unity's existence is a necessary condition.

Thus, there is nowhere visible any source of new productivity due to the War, from the yield of which the burdens of war indebtedness could be borne; and all the greater is the loss of substance. Today the victor States still imagine that they can balance this loss of substance in the books of their national economic systems by means of their claims under the debt agreements. They will have to make up their minds to write the loss of substance off their national fortunes, and to revise the claims of their creditors from that standpoint. In no other way will they be able to bring their books and therewith the world's trade into order.

Chapter Six

DEMARCATION

We have arrived at our result purely on the basis of the given facts, simply seeking the connexion between cause and effect, and not allowing ourselves to be influenced by any sort of political postulate or program. Before we go on to consider the conclusions to be drawn from our result, let us pause to take the bearings of our result between the various views of what is and the various programs of what should be.

CAPITALIST EMBARRASSMENT

That all those who have formed theories of their own about the crisis—and what economist has not done so by now?—should declare our argument unsound is too human to call for special notice. Bernard Shaw showed in *The Doctor's Dilemma* how each one bases his diagnosis on the special branch of medicine which he claims as his own, and regards every other diagnosis as bosh. Why should it be otherwise with the physicians of economic life?

That does not prevent an equal number of other critics from declaring that what the writer has to say is all perfectly familiar and old history. "That debts prove burdensome, that a country in debt is worse off than a country out of debt, that the last war in particular left behind it an enormous burden of debt, all this everybody knows. What is the writer getting at? Does he want to plead for the so-and-soth time for the remission of debts? There is no need for him to spend all this energy, just for that, in setting out a calculation that is thoroughly familiar already to the experts."

If it is all nothing new, so much the better. In that case the practical conclusions which we shall draw will so much the more easily find acceptance, and so many the more will there be to work for their practical application. For it was neither ambition nor the desire to spring something new on the world that prompted the author of this book to write, but simply concern for the fate of us all.

In the list of causes drawn up by the International Chamber of Commerce, war indebtedness is mentioned quite late, in the last place but one, when the reader is already quite sure that the ten factors already adduced have thoroughly sufficed to bring about the crisis; it is, moreover, mentioned only indirectly in the form of the taxes that have to be raised to meet it. Its mention at all in this form shows the recognition of the first link in the chain of causes, and for not a few readers who still regard our argument with a certain doubt and scepticism this will be a confirmation. But the recognition of causes stops short at that first link. There is not a word to give war debts first place among the causes of the crisis as the determining factor through which post-war trade and industry differ fundamentally from pre-war. Let us gladly recognize that the International Chamber of Commerce even seems to have thought of the internal indebtedness and not only of the political external indebtedness, for it speaks of "unprecedented *national* and international indebtedness." But there is no word about their interreactions or even about their relative magnitude. Not a word about the war debts being unproductive debts, unlike the pre-war public debts. Not a word about the pressure of taxation being only one aspect of the debt service, with the liberation of interest and amortisation as its other aspect—moneys that are first withdrawn from the economic system through the taxation service; withdrawn, moreover, from consumption. Not a word about the public debt service setting free that extra capital of which the "ill-judged outlay" is regarded today by competent observers as exclusively or very substantially responsible for the economic depression. The emphasis in our consideration of the debts lies—be it repeated once more—on the fact that the debts are not regarded merely as debts—that is, as the debtor's liabilities—not even only as debts and also, to carry their effect a further step on, a taxation burden, but in their whole economic function.

At this point some business critics will say that the difference between productive and unproductive debt, which is the crucial point in the author's whole argument, is, from a commercial point of view, rank dilettantism, to use no worse phrase. "Debts are debts, and debts have to be paid back; that is the central pillar of the business code. If a bank opens a credit for a company, and the managing director spends the money on his mistress or on political propaganda, is the company's liability to repay the loan any less because the managing director has spent the money unproductively?"—Certainly it is not. But if the company goes bankrupt because of this unproductive expenditure, the bank will nevertheless lose some of its money. Whether the company gets into difficulties through the unproductive expenditure will depend—assuming it to be otherwise in a sound condition—upon the relative magnitude of the managing director's unproductive expenditure and of the productively employed share capital. Be it observed also that the repayment liability of a private undertaking has its natural limit in the amount of its own capital. More than its own capital a private undertaking cannot lose; it may bring down unfortunate creditors in its fall, but a beneficial limit is set in the last resort to the effect of the unproductive conduct of a business. For the repayment liability of a State, on the other hand, this beneficial limit of its own capital does not exist, because the State usually has no capital of its own—apart from, perhaps, a few enterprises run under business conditions, and its landed property. Its essential asset is its citizens' taxable capacity. The measure of its liability for repayment is, however, bound up with its authority. Since the regulative factor of private business, the fact that its unproductive debts have to be measured against its productive share capital, is lacking to the State, and since the State's own authority is involved in the debts, the State tends to make use of its asset, the taxable capacity of its citizens, to the uttermost limit, to the extent even of itself injuring this asset through levies on property (for these are no longer payments of taxes, but of taxable capacity itself), before admitting to itself that the repayment of its unproductive debts has a limit in the productivity of its citizens' trade and industry, just as in the case of private undertakings. No undertaking can repay unproductive debts beyond the limit of its productive power; and this simple proposition is true also of world trade and industry.— Is it the dawning of this realization that leads, for instance, Felix Pinner to write as follows in the *Berliner Tageblatt* of October 3, 1931? Help, he writes, can only come "within the framework of a great world settlement, in connexion with which the rich countries must resign themselves to a healthier distribution of gold and therewith the restoration of sound currencies, with the object of overcoming the great world deflation."

But is it not undermining the authority of a State to propose that the treatment of State loans should depend on whether the money subscribed was applied productively or unproductively? Does not the authority of the State stand beyond that distinction? Is not the authority of the State incorporated in civil law in its credit? And is the author, who makes play with such a distinction, perhaps a Bolshevist?

More as to that immediately. But first let us show from one more example how closely capitalist thinking is approaching the writer's position. In the leading article of the commercial section of the *Frankfurter Zeitung* of October 4, 1931 the present crisis is characterized as a "self-deflation, coming into operation without any active throttling policy on the part of the note banks. In the world today we have to do with a self-shrinkage of this sort, coming into play without the intervention of the note banks." Since the word "inflation" has become part of every German's vocabulary, the various compounds of "-flation" have become fashionable. Any deflation implies a preceding inflation, a swelling up above the normal. But what was it that had been inflated? Before the present crisis broke out, before 1929, had anyone mentioned that world trade was suffering from the inflation of anything and needed to be brought back to normal through a self-deflation? At that time people were talking of prosperity, considered that all was in order, and believed in the practicability of the "normal years" of the Young Plan annuities. Nevertheless, the sentence quoted is entirely right, only the step is missing to the recognition of what exactly it is that is inflated. There is only the statement of what the note banks have *not* done: the excesses of the balance of payments in America and France are "neither being used in the country itself for an extension of the circulation of money, nor applied to the export of capital. The consequence is a gigantic accumulation of gold. . . ." The reader will see at once: that is, once more, pure Strakoschism. The gold façade is seen as it is and taken for what it is, but nothing is asked as to how it got there. The riddle is not solved by the cunning talk of "self-deflation." After all, even a deflation does not come about by spontaneous generation. And even to say "self-ignition" is to pose a question as to origin. What is not noticed is that what was inflated, and still is, is the war-time accumulation of debt; that these debts kept relatively quiet so long as they merely stood in the books and were collected relatively gently; but that, so soon as the collection was taken up seriously and in full measure, they were bound to weigh on productive capital with all the burdensomeness of a watering of stock.

THE MARXISTS

The Bolshevists are laughing at it all. For them it was long ago a settled matter that the capitalist system of world trade and industry is doomed to collapse, and they will at best have a compassionate smile for the way the writer is fidgeting in the outer precincts of Marxist revelation.

In reply to all this crowing, it may be pointed out that Marx predicted the collapse of the capitalist order through the process of private capitalist production, and not through the accumulation of State indebtedness.

But that is not all. Even if the unity of world trade were to be sundered by the overburdening of productive capital with the unproductive war indebtedness, that does not in the slightest degree upset the basic fact of the capitalist system, the fact that 100 marks at January 1, if they are employed in economic production, are equivalent to 105 marks at December 31; whereas if they are unproductively expended or consumed, at December 31 they will have disappeared. Let us not be told that this is an equivocation because the conditional clause "if they are employed in economic production" begs the whole question of private capitalism. This basic fact is, on the contrary, the symbolic representation of the growth of all trade and industry. The fact exists, quite independently of whether it is recognized by humanity or not, and still more independently of whether humanity accepts it as the basis of its economic system or not. It exists so surely as in all ages men have behaved in one quarter productively and in another unproductively.

Until the dawning of the capitalist age this fact was not systematically exploited; in the Middle Ages the Church tried to abrogate it; the State can turn against it by taxing interest out of existence, and so on. All this makes no difference to the fact that the basic fact of capitalism (or, more simply, the function of capital) exists as surely as a number "exists." For it is nothing but a metrical relationship, it expresses nothing but the fact that it relates the return from an activity to the original implement of this activity, and and so makes it plain whether this activity—in the economic field—was productive or not.

The Bolshevists may be satisfied that all this has no application to their order of society. (We will waste no words on the fact that they regard all State trafficking with debts as an evil, irrespective of the origin of the debts, and as a means of providing incomes for a privileged class.) All that does nothing to alter the fact that they are only able—for the present—to balance their State budget by having forests cut down for the growth of which Nature expended the energy of centuries, and having them cut down by exported workers whose labours they organize terroristically.

In spite of compulsion of this sort, the Bolshevists are unable to achieve an equilibrium in their balance of payments. The Soviet Republic is, in fact, very far from being a "self-contained economic area"—it does not even give our ideologues that satisfaction. The Russian trade figures for the first six months of 1931 showed an adverse balance of 152,000,000 roubles on an import total of 518,000,000 roubles, a circumstance that is providing anxieties enough for our Reichsbank (the German Reichsbank is, of course, the only note bank which has Russian bills in hand).

For the present the "capitalist inducement" (which presupposes unequal rewards) is still the cheapest relay horse for every economic activity—and, as everybody knows, Stalin not long ago reintroduced unequal remuneration of labour. Where this inducement is absent or is deliberately dispensed with, there has to be either a great hierarchy of supervisors and consequently an extensive bureaucracy, which always brings up the cost of the final product, quite independently of whether it is calculated "capitalistically" or not—or else terrorism.

The moderate Marxists of the German Social Democratic type believe themselves to have found in the wage agreement the complete corrective of the private capitalist system. They are on the defensive, all their interest is concentrated on the maintenance of the wage agreement and industrial arbitration. It is nothing to them where capital is to find its income, so long as it allows the worker to participate under the agreement in the yield of production. It has entirely escaped their observation that rationalization was one long technical attack on the wage agreement—not on the individual claims under the agreement, but on the number of claims—after every legal attack had been made impossible by the strength of the workers' organizations. On the contrary, with their fixed concentration on the level of wages, they have even helped to promote rationalization, through the theory that increases in wages stimulate technical progress and are accordingly productive. The final report of the German Commission of Inquiry shows expressly how the policy of the trade unions contributed to the excessive application of rationalization and the intensifying of capital outlay.

Firmly holding on to their wage agreement, they are compelled helplessly to watch the number falling day by day of those for whom industry is able to provide any employment at all under the agreement, and to watch the voters abandoning them under the influence of a mood of which they are unable to divine the cause.

THE FASCIST MOOD IN GERMANY

It has often enough been said that the program of the German National Socialists is not altogether a model of clarity of thought. The more remarkable is it that this absence of clear thinking in no way diminishes the recruiting power of the party. This party does not grow through the communication of abstract propositions and theories, as Marxism did through the labours of generations, but is fed by a mood. If one wants to track down the mystery of this party, one must discover the source of this mood. It is a definite "anti-" mood. This mood is directed on one hand against the Communists, though not so much against their teachings as against the members of the Communist Party personally. Perhaps no one is really competent to judge this mood who has not worked at the bench alongside Communists. It is the same mood that brought the success of the Fascist Party in Italy. Personal as the mood is in this aspect, its other aspect is purely abstract. It is directed against an unknown, impersonal power which can only be approximately described: against "international capital," against the "stock exchange," and so on. As a mood cannot live for ever on an abstraction, but needs a precipitate of the concrete, the concrete figure of the "Jews" has been adopted. Here the adequacy of the concrete illustration to express the idea to be conveyed is about the same as that of the famous definition which set out to sum up all humanity by describing man as a "featherless two-legged animal"—for, after all, there is "a measure of truth" in that definition. Nobody believes that this "anti-" complex is meant to be directed against "the Jews personally," except the Jews themselves, in so far as they are afraid of it. Primitive as the National Socialists are in many things, their mood is able to make a distinction of persons here. For if it were as simple as all that, if they were concerned only with "the Jews personally," they would have available the weapon of a quiet boycott of the Jewish retailers, a weapon which certainly would not be ineffective when brought to bear by so numerous a party, and which they could apply without having to wait for a revolution or a parliamentary majority. At the time of the former Ahlwardt Party the mood may have had this personal, *petit bourgeois* element, and a similar undercurrent of personal animosity may be present among the "Nazis," but the essence of the mood is directed this time along other, impersonal lines. It is concerned with something "behind" the Jews, a super-personal power or a system, of which the Jews are merely—at a fairly high percentage rate—representatives. It is not great possessions, and not plutocracy, not class domination and not "capitalism" in the Marxist sense. What, then, is it? The movement has never been able to give a precise and concrete formulation of what it is troubled about in this direction.

"But how can the writer make such a statement as that? Has not the 'breaking of the bondage to interest' been in the program of the movement from its earliest days?" But it is precisely at this point that the naïveté of the conception is most painfully obvious. The engineer Feder, who regards himself as the discoverer of "bondage to interest" and has in truth discovered nothing but the simple fact that interest is paid on money lent, attacks every sort of interest on loans, on moral grounds, and is in no way distinguishable in this respect from the Bolshevists. That from this position the whole economic system of the Bolshevists would have necessarily and inevitably to be accepted is a logical conclusion which has been escaped by not thinking the position out with all that logic. Nor is any other suggestion offered as to how, after interest has been abolished, trade and industry are to go on. When the Walchensee loan was issued in Munich, Feder called a meeting there and protested against the loan; a work of this sort belonged to the people and must not be delivered up to the power of capitalist lenders. As a means of getting the work executed, he made the suggestion in all sincerity that the workers should be paid in State assignats. Feder has never got beyond this level of helpfulness with his "Federgeld," his feather money. What the fate of his "non-interest-bearing Treasury bonds" would be, he can learn when he will from the history of the French Revolution, if he objects to recognizing the inflation in Germany as pointing any moral because it took place under a "Marxist" system of government. How his "feather money" is to be preserved from sharing the fate of all token currency, from falling, namely, into depreciation—which means in practice that the worker paid with it has to bear the loss—is a question which Feder has never succeeded in answering.

Since the party turned to constitutionalism, it has been decidedly less vocal on the subject of breaking the bondage to interest. But it would be quite a mistake to infer that the impossibility of this demand has been recognized by the party leadership. Hans Reupke (of the Federation of German Industry) tried to represent it as dead and buried as thoroughly as the groups with whom he is associated would like it to be. In a pamphlet called *Der Nationalsozialismus und die Wirtschaft* (*National Socialism and the Economic System*), he claimed that the demand for the breaking of the bondage to interest was out of date; that it had been "introduced into the movement at an earlier period." This pamphlet was promptly disowned by Hitler. Meanwhile Franz Hochstetter, in a pamphlet called *Leihkapital und Goldwährung als Grundlagen der Geldversklavung in Deutschland* (*Loaned Capital and Gold Currency as the Bases of*

Enslavement by Money in Germany), has declared war anew on loan capital as uncompromisingly as ever and has associated the rebellion with the National Socialist theory of money (Heft 26 of the Nationalsozialistische Bibliothek, published by Feder).

We thus have the following curious state of things: the party is fed on an "anti-" complex, but is unable itself to describe clearly what it is that it is out to fight. In the abstract the purpose of the party is described as to wage war against loaned capital, a purpose purely and simply Bolshevistic; yet the Bolshevists are the very enemy against whom the National Socialists are doing battle every day.

Some readers may perhaps have imagined that they recognized the National Socialist theorem of "bondage to interest" in our thesis. But a glance at the actual position will show how far that is from being the case. We have described the war debts as unproductive for the very reason that we take our stand on the capitalist basis of productivity, and because in our opinion the one of all things most needful is the liberation of productive capital from the pressure of unproductive debts. The National Socialists attack every sort of interest on loaned capital on moral grounds, without concerning themselves about productivity.

They do, in point of fact, make a distinction—they respect immobile capital and only attack the mobile loan capital. There is a touch in this of agrarian romanticism, as though feudal capital could do no wrong and as though it were a higher form of service to administer one's own property—or to let it fall into ruin. The National Socialist movement thus occupies exactly the opposite pole to the emancipation movement of a hundred and fifty years ago. Then the middle-class movement for freedom of activity was struggling (under the leadership of Baron vom Stein, whom the National Socialists paradoxically claim as their forefather) against the restrictions through which feudal capital prevented the free exercise of a trade, hampering the development of the whole economic system of the country. Today National Socialism is fighting in the name of immobile capital against the "injustice" of interest on loaned capital. The amount of injustice which the feudal economic order represented is forgotten. So short is man's memory, so quickly does a movement turn into its opposite. That would not matter so much were it not also forgotten that what is being worked for formerly existed as a lower stage of economic development, and that its achievement would of necessity mean retrogression to an economic level of the past.—We have considered the question strictly within the capitalist mechanism of productivity and profit-earning capacity, and within the gold currency system. The National Socialists imagine that they can introduce an entirely different system of production, away from "enslavement by loaned capital," through a "currency reform."

Great as this difference of ideas is, we are sure that

the Fascist mood—and we saw that this party is to be comprehended rather from the point of view of a mood than of ideas—is in a very high percentage degree the product of the economic pressure which proceeds from the war indebtedness, and not simply the pressure of loan capital. This can be shown negatively: the mood is directed not against the "ruling classes," not against the "bourgeoisie"—the National Socialist soul is a thoroughly bourgeois one—not against the "capitalist class." In private dealings no National Socialist sees any harm in interest being paid for a loan—not even Herr Feder, member of the Reichstag, himself, if the story of his concern about his bank deposit is true. The influx into the ranks of the National Socialist Party is due, in the case of most of those who give the party the power of numbers, to the feeling, as under a secret fear of some superhuman power, that things could not be worse. So long as the economic pressure of the war indebtedness continues, the influx into the party will also continue.

The inference, for all who are concerned to combat the growth of the party, is that it will be best combated by stopping up the source of the mood; that is, by mitigating the pressure of the debt. So long as this is impossible, there will be little success in the contest with the party. For a mood cannot be got rid of by argument, only by the removal of the cause of the mood; this consideration is true also of the soul of man in politics.

The National Socialists will deride this as a platitude. Reduction of the pressure of the debts—the others will never get that, only they themselves, the National Socialists, will get it. Have they not for whole years past been the loudest denouncers of the tribute payments?

But their denunciation proceeds only from the national point of view, and thus develops at once into an attitude of hostility to the creditors. It considers also, for the same reason, only the external political indebtedness. Not a moment's thought is given to the consideration that the creditor States are themselves in debt, and to many times the extent of the foreign debts. Not a moment's thought is given to the consideration that from this point of view there should actually be a possibility of producing a solidarity between the various productive classes in debtor and creditor countries—although this consideration might very naturally have lain ready to hand for the believers in "bondage to interest." Not a moment's thought is given to the fact that there is, after all, something that stands above the economic egoisms of the nations, something in which all participate actually in the midst of these egoisms—the productivity of world trade as a whole. It would certainly have been possible to open up from this point of view an incomparably more fruitful international discussion than from the mere position of protest against the creditors.

But, strangely enough, the union of the Fascist

mood with economic insight seems, for the present, still to be confined to the land of the birth of Fascism. Why do not the German National Socialists pursue the simple path of taking lessons from Signor Mussolini, whom they so admire? Italy is certainly having her taste of the crisis, but amid all his power Mussolini has never entertained the idea of mitigating it by going off the gold standard. On the contrary, at the very time when speculation has been trying to nibble at all the currencies, he has been protecting the gold lira with the utmost energy. He has often enough expressed in unmistakable terms his views on war indebtedness and the Young Plan. But he has never dreamed of making them into an ideology directed against all loaned capital; he has negotiated instead for his country. He engaged the sympathies of the creditor countries at an early date for Italy, who had just made good her escape from Bolshevism, and secured such good terms that one may almost say that Italy pays virtually no interest (up to 1940 only ⅛th per cent!), merely paying back the principal.—In the Fascist Corporative Constitution capital and labour are alike subordinated to the corporations—at least in theory—of which Mussolini holds the threads (Mussolini has a right of veto against all resolutions of the corporations). So far Mussolini's authority has kept down the antagonisms which doubtless exist. In practice Mussolini has often enough shown that he assesses the value of capital according to the practical significance it has for labour in any concrete case;

and that, accordingly, he subordinates the income of capital to productive labour and not the other way round. He has not shrunk from compelling employers by forcible means to keep their works going, irrespectively of their profit-earning capacity, when this seemed to him to be desirable in the interests of labour.

That the valuation of capital will have to depend in the future on the function it fulfils for the productivity of the economic system, and that in this there lies the last possibility of saving capitalism—this Mussolini has realized. In Germany there is a great deal of talk about State capitalism, so soon as the State has to come to the aid of a bank in difficulties. But the parties that are tussling for dominance in the State show as yet little clear conception of how the relationship between State and capital is to be brought to a new fruitfulness. Either one finds a rigid adherence to the old article of faith that State debts are an abstract something of which the income is inviolable, and that the question out of what that income is to be earned cannot be allowed to be raised; or, among the extremists of Right and Left alike, war is declared against any sort of interest on capital on purely ideological grounds, as if it were possible to banish from the world by a simple decree the eternal fact of the function of capital.

From one quarter alone we hear words that raise hopes of a realization of the facts such as is here advocated. We imagine that the words are to be understood in that sense which Dr. Brüning used in his speech to the German bankers on June 27, 1931, and which we have set in front of this book as motto:

"Unless all the signs are deceiving us, we are living in a period in which, if the existing system of trade and industry is to be preserved from grave and lasting convulsions, it is necessary to introduce a broader and more generous conception of the idea of capital."

General as is the phraseology of this sentence, it does at least say this: that the rigid conception of capital as something affecting only the rights of the individual, something with two aspects only—on this side the capital provided by the creditor, on that the interest paid by the debtor—is no longer tenable, and that it will have to give way before a more elastic conception; out of sheer necessity.

This dictum of Brüning's has not been fully discussed by a single organ of his party; consequently we are unable to judge how far he spoke only for himself. In any case, it is a forward-looking pronouncement, and it will shortly give us fresh occasion for consideration. Here we merely wanted to demarcate our thoughts in relation to the opinions organized in the power-groups of the parties.

FALLING BETWEEN ALL THE STOOLS

The result of our demarcation is that we seem to fall between all the stools.

Our thesis was that for public debts of the magnitude of the war indebtedness it is not a matter of indifference whether they are productive or unproductive debts; for the simple reason that the interest on these debts does not grow out of nothing, but has to be set apart out of the yield of productive capital. If from this position we regard the attitude of the various party groups, we find:

1. The middle-class parties of the Centre, including the moderate Socialists, put productive and unproductive debts on the same footing, recognizing both; they do not ask where the income comes from for the unproductive debts; and they look on helplessly with folded hands at the menace to the living capital from the burden of the dead debt and at the shrinking up of trade and industry;

2. the Marxist extremists on the Left put productive and unproductive debts on the same footing, rejecting both; they regard all income from capital as a class injustice and are convinced that they can eliminate it by means of a changed order of society;

3. the National Socialist extremists on the Right put productive and unproductive debts on the same footing, attacking both as bondage to interest; some of them believe that they could set up an economic system freed from all bondage to interest by means of a changed currency; others simply feel the burden of war indebtedness apart from any ideas on the subject and believe that they could throw it off by cutting their country's economic system off from that of the world's trade.

The startling result of this summary is that all three

of the main political groups, the Centre and the Right and Left extremists alike, have their several views on capitalism and yet fail, all three of them, to recognize the essential feature of capitalism.

They see only the interest on capital. But the interest on capital, important and at the same time mysterious as it is, is not the essential feature of capitalism. It is the feature only of the money-lender's capital, the old and by now phlegmatic form of capitalism. The essential feature of the whole system of the capitalism that is conqueror and ruler of the world is productivity, an impersonal process, soulless or even cruel in ways that have often been described, and so impersonal that it is attributed only to capital itself, and we all use the phrase that would have seemed nonsense in past centuries: "Capital produces." The interest on capital is only the measure of this productivity; it is a purely relative measure and not quantitative, as all capitalist productivity is relative and not quantitative. The capitalist measures by the productivity of his undertaking, and by its inner reserves, whether it is "well" or "ill," not by the dividend.

Anyone who misses this fundamental meaning of capitalism, anyone who demands an income for unproductive capital just as if it were productive, injures the capitalist system and reduces its vitality. For the system is dependent on the principle of selection which derives directly from the principle of productivity (and is at the same time a confirmation of that principle), and which runs as follows: the less productive capital must give way before the more productive.

Thus the continuance of the capitalist system is threatened simultaneously on all sides—not only from the extremist wings, its declared enemies, but also from the middle-class Centre parties, who imagine themselves its chief defenders; by these latter for the reason that they overstrain the principle of the earnings of capital, demanding earnings where there is no productivity.

The Bolshevists know this. They imagine themselves to have discovered that capitalism is toppling over, and base on that their confidence that time is working for them, and that the victory cannot slip from their grasp.

Chapter Seven

PRACTICAL CONCLUSIONS

With the discovery of the cause, the task we set ourselves is accomplished. We asked what barrier had thrust itself between want and superfluity and was preventing their equation. Now we know why it is that no fructifying current is flowing along the fall of potential from superfluity to want, turning the mills of industry and trade, but, on the contrary, the difference of potential between want and superfluity only grows constantly greater, while at the same time the current of economic turnover continues to dwindle.

Our purpose was "to discover how the facts hang together, and to leave it at that." The conclusions which we shall try, in what follows, to draw from our result make no difference to the result itself or to its rightness or wrongness. The reader will, accordingly, keep his criticism of the result independent of whether he finds these conclusions drawn from it sensible or absurd, practicable or visionary.

PROGNOSIS

Prophesying is always a ticklish business, but if one believes oneself to have discovered the cause, one cannot escape the obligation of giving a prognosis.

We recognized the crisis as a crisis of capital deflation. If this is right, it follows that the crisis will not begin to pass until the surplus dead capital of world trade and industry has been got rid of. Until, in other words, there is nothing left standing in the books of the world economic system that has no actual existence. Every business man who wants to set a sick undertaking on its feet knows that the very first thing needed is to get the valuation right in the books and to write off all that had an existence in the more prosperous past, but has none any longer. Is it so difficult to learn the same truth for world trade and industry?

If this process of deflation is not deliberately steered for—and as yet its existence is not even recognized—it will take a very long time. We shall have then to prepare for a long trial of endurance. Wagemann and his long waves will have won through; only we make this prophecy not on the basis of historic analogy, but on that of an insight into the mechanism. The downward curve of the wave will continue as much longer as the post-war debts exceed those of the Napoleonic wars in relation to productive capital—Europe's then, the world's now. That does not exclude the possibility of smaller waves being superposed on this downward curve as "interim booms."

But will world trade, will the world's economic system, survive this process of deflation at all? If the elimination of the capital that can no longer be carried is left to the free play of forces that for a long time past have no longer been free, the process of elimination will be extraordinarily painful. There will be nothing for it but to witness the collapse of many more enterprises which have failed to recognize their actual situation, nursing the illusion that present conditions are "temporary." As that elimination continues, the turnover of the firm of World Trade will shrink up further. Whether the process will be accompanied by the further withdrawal of one or another member from the firm depends in the last resort on the personal element—was not the Bolshevist Revolution carried through by an extraordinarily small number of men? All that can be said in general is that the point at which withdrawal from the world's economic system will be considered the preferable course seems to depend on the relative magnitude of the unproductive debts. Anyone who does not admit this connexion will find a proof of it in the fact that, whenever the question arises of accepting the Soviet Republic into the circle of capitalist States, the question of the recognition of the old war debts is made a condition. Russia's flight into Bolshevism took place when the pressure of the war indebtedness had become unendurable. There seems to be a law that when the pressure of public debts reaches a certain point, it becomes preferable to take refuge in Bolshevism, much as at the moment when leather prices attain a certain level, the shoes outside the bedroom doors in the hotels inevitably begin to be stolen.

Some god or devil beyond the clouds of world history could thus produce at any time just as much Bolshevism on the earth as he chose; he would only need to raise the debt pressure in the State concerned to the requisite level.

It would be the greatest paradox in world history if the function of that devil were to be taken over, of all countries, actually by Puritan America, and if, by her stubborn insistence on placing productive and unproductive capital on the same footing, she were to fulfil Marx's prophecy, which even the Marxists long ago revised, in a way Marx himself never dreamed of.

IS CAPITALISM SAWING ITSELF OFF ITS BRANCH?

Here we pause at the question which is exercising the minds of so many Germans, some intellectuals, some not: Is not this an inevitable development? Has not the die perhaps been cast? Does any chance still remain of steering clear of this development?

Let us consider the course by which it all came: The War threw out of operation the brake which sets limits in a healthy economic system to the formation of new capital, the brake provided by the fact that only so much new capital comes into existence as can be permitted to branch off from the yield of production. In that spirit our forefathers saved. The regulator of saving-activity lay in the rate of interest that could be secured by capital. Before the War a slow but very steady decline in the rate of interest on capital was clearly to be observed. With the War everything was suddenly altered. To begin with, the State at once raised the rate of interest, for it needed a great deal of money. Where before the War could five per cent be got for State loans that were trustee securities? The State lavished on the population, in the form of army contracts, the moneys thus brought in, and the population returned them to the State in the form of fresh loans; but loans burdened with the obligation to pay fresh rates of interest. Meanwhile the State went guarantee that the money lent to it should not be robbed of its interest by other and more active capital. The loan paper piled up. Suddenly the universal recipe seemed to have been discovered for everyone to become propertied. The word "inflation" had not then been invented. Germany made its acquaintance only for currency inflation, and then only at a time when her currency was already falling. The American citizen has not to this day the faintest idea that the prosperity whose return he so ardently desires was an after-effect of the war-time inflation. How everything came then, how people sought desperately for means of squeezing an income out of the extra capital of the war indebtedness, as though it were healthy, productively employed capital, and how to this end the only recourse known to the capitalist was resorted to, that of the increase of production—all this has been described here at length. The original sin lay in believing that healthy, interest-bearing capital could be produced without the diligent saving and putting-into-the-business of our forefathers, in lending the State what had been drawn from the State itself through the mechanism of the war economy—or even lending what was going to be drawn. People were proud of this circulation, spoke of the War "supporting itself," and gave no thought to the fact that there was nowhere to be found any point of productivity in this circulatory process which could justify the payment of interest.

Is there not a deep irony in the development now, after so many years, of all this through the crisis into its opposite? In the crisis, which arose through an undue stretching of the principle of the earning of interest by capital, leading to a condition in which even healthy money declines to bring in interest? If France refrains from building up capital to the full measure of the money in her vaults and exporting it, that means that she prefers to do without the income from exporting the capital. France, the classic country of the capitalist *rentier*, is suddenly behaving as uncapitalistically as an Indian prince who heaps up gold in his treasury. And it is this country that, in following this course, is doing best in the present situation. Already the neutrals, Switzerland, Holland, are hurrying to change their gold credits into pure gold. Gold is perpetually on the move on a scale never before known. The return from the investment no longer counts, security is everything.

In such a revulsion from the overstraining of the

principle of investment income, is not a deep vengeance being exacted? But will the revulsion stop in mid course? Will it not lead actually to all income from invested capital ceasing and the Bolshevist economic system coming into being? And will "God suffer this vengeance to be taken from him"?

THE FORCE OF ROUTINE

Let us not be suspected of purposing at the last moment to turn moralist and to lay aside economic considerations in order to deliver a homily if we reply: after every transgression there is opportunity for reflection. We are speaking only of economic reflection.

The principal article of faith of the capitalist bourgeoisie is contained in the postulate that debts shall be paid back with due interest. On this dogma hangs the whole capitalist order; in the bill-of-exchange process with all its horrible abstractness it has found its legal precipitate. To lose credit is for the man who works on his capital much the same misfortune as for a Chinese to lose face. The merchant who shoots himself over his ledger because his firm has failed wins much the same respect as the captain who goes down with his ship rather than leave her as she founders. It makes no difference to our point that people have learnt in our day to think much more laxly of these things. We are speaking of the classical capitalism.

If anyone quarrels with that proposition, is he not already a Bolshevist?

And yet that proposition is not the ultimate one, but only a corollary. It is the corollary, turned into an imperative, of the proposition which now does really rule capitalist economy, the law of productivity, which contains the basic fact of capitalism and which we have formulated thus: that 100 marks at January 1, if they are employed in economic production, are equivalent to 105 marks at December 31.

We said at the time that the conditional clause "if they are employed in economic production" contains no equivocation, that we were not trying to use it to beg the whole question of the capitalist economic system. The proposition is valid irrespectively of the particular economic order existing at any time, just as it was certainly valid before ever the capitalist system was discovered and elaborated. It was valid when the Church laid its veto on usury, wherever a man could borrow a hundred marks and apply or consume them productively. And even if all money were abolished, it is possible either to apply as an implement or else to consume the product of the labour of a man whose services have been borrowed. The economic order can do no more, at the most, than determine whether a lender of 100 marks shall be permitted to demand the whole or part of the 5 marks for himself, and the law of productivity has nothing to do with that. The law of productivity is thus valid in all cases, independently of the economic order, and the economic order has no place in the conditional clause. What is in the conditional clause is something quite different—the freedom of the individual.

It is only because of the existence and the familiarity of the law of productivity that it is possible for the capitalist economic order to think of demanding interest for debts. But this order has forgotten that the law of productivity contains the conditional clause: "if they are employed in economic production." When it lays down the law of interest as absolute, it eliminates the conditional sentence as inapplicable; in other words, it lays down the absolute law: *"Thou shalt only incur debts for productive purposes."* And this is indeed the supreme law of the good capitalist patriciate. Anyone who runs up debts for unproductive purposes is despised for "living beyond his means," as though he were already on the brink of bankruptcy.

A few hundred years ago all this was quite different. The law of productivity existed, but it was not yet known and was not the standard of labour. All that was known was the productivity of the soil. Money was regarded as a dead thing, no more capable of bearing fruit than a stone. Then the townsmen, who were just as pious people as the citizens of the capitalist patriciate, observed the law of the Church: "Thou shalt take no interest."

Relatively young as capitalism still is, it has already entirely forgotten the conditional nature of the law of productivity on which its whole system rests. It is the force of routine that has taught it this forgetfulness. Every day every bill that comes in drives home the idea that the obligation of interest is something abstract, and that the question of the employment of the capital must not be asked.

This power of routine to get itself taken for granted, this power of man's own devices to win for themselves an independent existence and, as impersonal matters of routine, to run away with their devisers, even succeeding at times in turning their original intention into its opposite, is a phenomenon that regularly recurs in world history, not merely an invention introduced by us to save our thesis. If we wanted to deal here in the history of civilization, we could adduce a whole list of examples. Money, to begin with; originally functioning as a medium of exchange and payment, it has long gone beyond this and made itself independent. Or, to take an example of an entirely different order, marriages, where the admissibility of dissolution of marriage puts into people's minds the idea of playing at divorce or even making a serious business of it. Anyone who is not satisfied with these examples may perhaps be convinced by the poet's reference to the good deed that became a plague.

It is only too true that the good deed of the gift of credit for production, through which in a few centuries the productive powers of humanity's economic system have been brought to an undreamed-of development, has been turned, by its routine application to war financing, into the horrible plague of the world crisis, which threatens to reduce these same productive forces at an equally rapid pace back to their first state. The volume of world trade has already been thrown back by decades; if things continue as at present, world trade will rapidly fall to the level of a hundred years ago: the blame will lie with the same forces which produced the development, only applied with a negative sign.

Because it is a matter of unquestioningly accepted routine that interest is paid for borrowed money, the State has incurred the heaviest debts in world history without taking thought for their interest-earning capacity, instead of financing the war from the beginning by taxation, as even Britain, for all her sense of responsibility, was only able to do in a very small degree. Who was responsible? The State was in difficulties. Shall one apply the logical argument which ends by blaming the murdered man for his murder? Did not the subscribers to the loans see the fact in front of their noses, that their money was not being invested for a productive purpose, and that the debts were growing to an amount on which it would never be possible to pay interest and amortisation without upsetting the equilibrium of the national economic system? Ah, presumably neither of the two was to blame. What was to blame was routine.

This routine is in the blood of all of us and prevents us from seeing clearly. Those who say in answer to the ideas of this book that "it is childish dilettantism to consider the question of productivity in connexion with State loans, for the interest service is guaranteed under all circumstances by the State," are placing routine above the living fact, for the fact is called Productivity. Those who say: "The writer is arguing as if the War was waged as a joint-stock enterprise, and the war loans issued as shares; in that case the question of productivity would be in place, but the obligation under State loans is abstract," are placing routine above the living fact, for the question is whence can the money for the debt service be produced, not what was the legal form in which the loans were issued.

This routine develops day by day its destructive power—destructive because it has been applied out of due season—and is in process of ruining world trade.

REFLECTION

Capitalism is on the straight road to ruin, because it has turned the routine of production against itself. As to that there is no doubt. The croakings of those who would like to begin digging its grave already are by no means premature rejoicings. The clock points to five minutes to twelve. Only a rapid decision can serve now.

Will capitalism liberate itself from the misapplication of dead routine and reflect on its own true nature? Will it once more remember, with the sense of responsibility of its forerunners, that its function and its only justification of existence is to serve productivity? That it is against its nature and beneath its dignity to draw interest from dead consumption?

Everyone knows the story of King Midas, who was doomed to die from hunger because his wish had been granted that everything should turn in his hands to gold. There go we ere long. Already capitalism, beginning to find no further opportunity of investment that offers security against loss in the crisis, can think of nothing better to do with its income than to turn it into gold. Constantly it is sending about gold transports, as a frightened cat carries her kittens. Only the tragedy is greater than in the old fable: with King Capitalism all those must also starve from whom he took the gold.

But is it any good to try to induce capitalism to reflect? When in a system routine has gained the mastery over the spirit, is that not the surest symptom of ossification, is it not the plainest signal that the time has come to get rid of the trouble by giving up the system? Has not capitalism brought down misery enough on humanity—taken the soul out of human relations, put machines in the place of living beings?

All that makes not the slightest difference to the elementary fact that we Germans are a people of sixty millions, living on a confined and ungenerous soil. The calculation that the soil of Germany could nourish eighty or a hundred millions may look well on paper. But the prophets of "autarchy," of self-sufficiency within her frontiers, must say how the forms of ownership are to be set up that would be essential to such intensive development. Does anyone suppose that these new forms of ownership could be set up without bloodshed?

But even if the readiness existed for such a change of ownership, there still remains the other condition of success: the conversion of the methods of the agricultural industry in Germany would demand an enormous expenditure of capital, which simply is not to be had.

Turn and twist as one may, the capitalist system is in any event the cheapest for Germany, if only because, to begin with, its apparatus is there to hand. The many economic prophets who demand a change of system for the very reason of our poverty forget the elementary fact that a conversion always costs money, that it presupposes a wealth of means of production and not a lack, and at the very least a wealth of soil, such as the Russians had. In so confined and overpopulated a country as Germany is, the Bolsheviks would have failed. They had to pass through a colossal destruction of money, through starvation and a retrogression almost to the level of the barter system; they were able to do this because their enormous country offers room at all times for a sort of simple exchange of natural produce; but, even so, millions starved to death. How would the conversion be likely to work out in a country whose economic system displays so complicated an apparatus as the German?

We will waste no time on those fanatics who want all this because they think that it is only in this way that the "New Birth" can come—as though the main thing about the phœnix were the ashes. These "cynics by ethos" should have had opportunities enough in the last seventeen years of considering the relations between destruction and construction. How many bitter pills the German people has already had commended to it under the chocolate coating of "new birth"! Other peoples speak of *rinascimento* when the mountains are really being scaled. Only the German nation has these cynics in the garb of Eulenspiegel, who are so keen to be on the climb that they revel in the sight of us all on the downward path. As if all that were not old history. We should really have learnt from Germany's past how much there is in the "renovating power of suffering." Did the German phœnix arise rejuvenated from the ashes of decades at the Peace of Westphalia? The strength for a new climb upwards had to be gathered in the course of generations, and from a very different source from the power of suffering.

Others are of a tamer ethos. They are not ambitious to go through the ravine of suffering, all that they want is to free economic life from the anarchy of egoisms. It must be conducted according to a "plan," and the plan must be placed in the hands of the State. That sounds very convincing. Only, strangely enough, the very people who want to see the supreme omnipotence in economic affairs vested in the State speak of the State in the same breath with utter contempt, if the actual, concrete State is meant, with its institutions of parliament and parties. The State of their dreams is everything, can do everything, knows everything; the actual State is a hopeless affair of "moribund parliamentarism," etc. Must a new State, then, be created? These ethicists will answer yes, without a moment's hesitation. But what assurance have we that the State of their dreams would not suffer in the process of realization that "falling away from the purity of the idea" which seems to be inseparable from all realization? It is literally the same confusion of thought from which the old Marxist Social Democracy suffered when it expected everything to come from the universal wisdom and universal care of the State, without considering whence the State was to draw all this wisdom and solicitude—until victory brought the demonstration that this trust in the State amounted to trust in an anæmic institutionalism. The people who talk so much of economic planning are already realizing—so far as they are not merely arm-chair ideologues—that it is easier to lay out than to carry out a plan. If the leaders of trade and industry in all their independence, with their own money or their living at stake, have made so many howlers, how many will they make when they only have to give their opinion in the seclusion and security of their offices as permanent officials and merely fractionally responsible members of an executive body?

The universally depreciated system of independent enterprise implies, after all, nothing more than that each individual business man is free to try all things, on penalty of losing his money or his capital if ever he misjudges a deal or an enterprise. Is any more promptly effective system conceivable? If a similar money penalty were suspended over the heads of administrative officials, what sort of a staff would that require?

Undoubtedly, independent enterprise may carry with it plenty of loss through the frictional effect of competition, but any restriction of enterprise would in all probability cost much more. For all such restrictions mean bureaucratization, and all bureaucratization adds to expense, since the costs of administration must always be borne by the final product. Apart from this, plenty of restrictions aimed at the reduction of the frictional effect grow out of the system of private enterprise itself. *These* have vitality, the State can reap the benefit of them. Restrictions imposed on trade and industry from without in the form of a "plan" invite automatic adjustment through corruption.

The ideologues are so fond of straightening out their ideas on paper, of establishing general principles, and give so little thought to the officials. The German State and municipal administrations are over-bureaucratized enough already; is it desired to over-bureaucratize the economic administration as well? That would be the surest way of bringing the German economic system to death from officialitis.

Because Germany is poor, and because freedom of enterprise in trade and industry is, after all, the cheapest system, Germany and her industries must hold fast to that system to the end, seriously as its existence is threatened—and the extent to which it is menaced from within can scarcely be painted in darker tones than has been done here. But to roll ourselves up in ourselves like a hungry hedgehog is a recourse still open to us.

THE REVERSED MACHINE

The period in which we are living is one of extraordinary tension. Reflect how long it is since men learned consciously to steer for productivity and to figure out the amount of their "capital." And it is only a century and a half ago that, after long struggles, freedom was won to give mobility to the means of production and to place them at pleasure wherever there was reason to hope for the maximum return. The result was a fructification of trade and industry such as had never before been dreamed of, so that today one must travel in non-capitalist countries in order to see degrees of poverty such as were formerly to be met with in our own country.

But already men have forgotten what the condition is of such productivity, already they have ceased to understand their own tool. As in past centuries they were unable to understand how a dead thing like money could bring in interest, so today they think that all money that is lent out must necessarily bring in interest out of itself, provided only that one takes the needful care to discover a "good" debtor, and what debtor could, surely, be better than the State? Thus today the world stands actually at the opposite pole to the Middle Ages.

And because men hold tenaciously to this belief, and because the State brings to bear all its forces to help to make this belief into reality, the whole process turns into its opposite. The routine idea of capitalism that capital brings in an income no longer effects an increase and extension of trade and industry, but effects a shrinkage. Already the progress, measured statistically, that the world had achieved since the War has been lost again. Day by day there is a rapid further retrogression. No one knows why. Some charge the technical progress that formerly was the object of their worship with having suddenly brought regress; others declare that the whole capitalist machine has gone to pieces and must be scrapped and thrown away as old iron. Yet the thing is so simple: the lever has been reversed, the machine has been set going backwards. It is, in truth, no real capital that has been invested in industry, and that ought now to be bringing in interest; it is only a nominal capital, with no actual existence at all. It has been calculated that for a fraction of the costs of the World War the Gulf Stream could have been deflected by a breakwater so that all central Europe could have had the climate of Meran. We will not discuss whether that feat of engineering would have been practicable; but, in any case, if the capital of the war loans had been so invested, *then* there would have been justification for demanding interest on it. Then, too, the war indebtedness would have produced no crisis.

Productively invested capital increases world trade; nominal capital with no real existence whatever, if it has to receive interest in the same way as productive capital, diminishes world trade—is not that proposition the simplest in the world?

Will the world grasp this, or is the legal complex of creditors' claims insurmountable? Will capitalism still have the energy to throw back the lever and set the machine going forward once more? Or has it already caught itself in the net of the interest claims, and will world trade be slowly but fatally throttled by its debts?

We will recall once more Dr. Brüning's dictum, that "it is necessary to introduce a broader and more generous conception of the idea of capital." If the rigid conception of private rights is held to, that debts are all alike debts, irrespectively of the economic employment of the money owed, the world will be ruined by the service of the war debts, ruined without chance of escape.

Who has energy and authority enough so to impress on the world the "broader and more generous" conception of the idea of capital that it is believed in and gives men the power to act rapidly?

The Americans came into the world as capitalistic people from the outset. Just as there is no mediæval cathedral in their country, so they have had no experience of the fact that at one time there was a prohibition of interest. One must, after all, make allowances for their failure to recognize the conditional nature of the law of productivity. Mr. Hoover's action was taken under the pressure of necessity; it had no deeper intellectual basis. Who will so provide this basis for the Americans that they all see it? Who will open their eyes and reveal to them that at present they are working the destruction of us all?

Perhaps it is a good thing that the German capitalist class lost its war loans. It is enabled thus to see the effect of the internal war indebtedness clearly and without the bias of egoism. Perhaps it is precisely in this that its vocation has been decided—to make clear to the world that world trade and industry can only be saved by restoring to capitalism its true justification; that the world's capital can only regain its strength if interest is paid only on productive capital and only out of its productive employment.

The Church, with its most ancient forefathers, always thought in due proportion in regard to the taking of interest; and the Church had from of old a greater freedom of outlook and capacity to see to the bottom of things. It cannot be difficult for Catholic thinkers to find here the categorical imperatives with which to approach the conscience of the world and to open its eyes to what its Anglican half is doing to it—for the service of the war debts is primarily an Anglo-Saxon affair.

The Protestant middle class, whose history is much more closely bound up with capitalism, faces these things at present without the elasticity of historic tradition. For that very reason it should take pains to familiarize itself with the true essence of capitalism and to save itself from becoming ossified through dead routine; for the doom of capitalism will be the doom of this class.

So far, however, there is no sign of any such familiarization in the capitalist classes of the world. They see only the façade of events and are interested only in little remedies for repairing the façade.

LITTLE REMEDIES

We have recognized the crisis as a crisis of deflation, or, perhaps better, to avoid that too hackneyed word, as a process of the elimination or reduction of capital; in any case, as a process of the reversal of the extension of indebtedness brought about by the economic conduct of the War. Since the element of deflation in the process is plain for all to see, and on the other hand people see only the monetary façade of the process, the idea has long ago been hit on that it might be possible to remedy the evil through currency inflation. As the word "inflation" has the worst of reputations in Germany, the process is also, under the influence of Herr Stegerwald, rather shamefacedly called "re-deflation." Those who are suggesting magic spells of this sort are not quite clear what it is exactly that should be deflated in the deflation, nor are they able to indicate how to deflate it. We have already mentioned the word "self-deflation" as an admission of the limit of knowledge.

"But," one or another reader may object, "is not the writer occupying the same position? Is not the deflation which he describes, the process of elimination of capital, equally a self-deflation? For what can be producing it? Certainly no policy of any note bank." At the risk of wearying other readers by replying to this objection—the deflation process of the elimination of capital is being assisted by the necessity of paying interest. Where the limit of the yield of interest is, there is the limit of capitalization. Conversely, capital is nothing but a claim to interest payment. To deflate bank-notes that bear no interest requires the application of pressure through the discount policy of the note banks. The war loans bear their rate of interest at the cost of deflationist pressure on all capital. Thus it was possible here to speak with justice of a "self-deflation."

Those remedies of inflation or re-deflation do, indeed, sound convincing: "We have been told that France is sterilizing gold. Why should the world allow that? If she is locking up the gold in her vaults, why does not the world go off gold? Then let France do what she will with her gold. If the currency is inflated, prices will rise and debts will fall, the countryman will rejoice, and everyone will be happy ever after."

Money is an interesting thing: it is the best of all examples of how stern virtue is and how beautiful is sin. Inflation leads to the abyss, and yet everyone has money. Deflation (properly so called; assuming, that is, that it has been preceded by inflation) is a process of recovery, and everyone is short of money.

Today in Germany there is this paradox, that the parties that imagine themselves to have the monopoly of moral excellence, Hugenberg and Hitler alike, are recommending the beautiful sin of inflation. But is it not more pleasant to sin with money than to starve for the sake of virtue?

Certainly gold is replaceable. Nowhere is it written that gold shall be the only currency metal.

But the question is not whether there shall be gold or not, but whether there shall be world trade or not. It is a question of the extent of acceptance. Gold is distinguished by nothing else but the fact that it is the world's currency metal.

Have people already forgotten the "inflation blockade"? What at the first moment is a premium on exports is at the second moment a raw-material blockade. The British example is inapplicable to Germany, because Britain buys her raw materials in the Empire. Has there not long been in Britain a strong movement for the closed system of Empire free trade? This movement has now come into possession of its own currency. These components of the British abandonment of the gold standard must not be lost sight of.

In Germany, after the short-lived joys of the revival through inflation, which would temporarily justify its advocates, there would come the long-drawn-out pains of the inflation blockade. For the parallel with sin exists also in the fact that the pleasure passes, the repentance lasts.

That is no mere silly jest, but is deep-rooted in the mechanism of inflation. The essence of inflation does not lie, as is generally supposed, in the increase of the quantity of money relatively to the basis of the currency (gold). That is not enough. Every inflation is a process which depends on *two* conditions: in addition to the increase of the money tokens there must be the fact that the credit of these tokens within the country is above the level corresponding to their increased quantity. The population must, so to speak, have failed as yet to notice or to grasp the fact of the increase of the token money. *Only on this span between objective quantity and subjective credit in the country of the money tokens does the "stimulating" effect of an inflation lie,* never in the mere quantity of the tokens. This effect is, in other words, an illusion under which the population labours with regard to the credit which it should attach to the currency. The German inflation lasted as long as it did because after the long years of peace it seemed inconceivable that "the German mark" should not be worth a mark. Once that span is eliminated, once the purchasing power of the money has changed to correspond with its quantity, there is an end of the stimulating effect of the inflation. Then all is as before within the country, only the external credit of the currency has been destroyed. The span lasts only a short time, the revision endures: thus does the pleasure of the sin pass, the repentance last.

If the stimulus of the inflation is to continue, the mass of the payment media must continually rush ahead of the internal credit, the note press must rotate continually more quickly. The parallel with sin is complete: once he has begun, man must go on and on in sin. There is no "controlled" inflation, even when so able a man as Mr. Keynes recommends it.

Those people in Germany who recommend inflation, with the important air of an apothecary's apprentice who has the key of the poison-chest, simply do not know that the objective increase in the currency is insufficient and that a psychological factor has to come into play in order to bring about the inflationary effect that they dream of. This time, however, in all probability this psychological factor would see to it in Germany that just the opposite should happen. The word "inflation" has in Germany a most sinister power, it is no longer a word, it is a demon, affecting everybody like a cry of "Poison gas!" If today the quantity of money were increased with the intention of producing inflation, in all probability the internal credit of this increase would not merely not lag behind it, but run ahead of it. The span would thus be in the opposite direction, and the inflation have exactly the opposite effect. This is no arbitrary supposition; the flight of the small middle class to the solid values of furniture and carpets during the last payment-medium crisis is proof of it. Indeed, the whole flight of German capital is nothing else but the discounting of a possible German inflation.

As a country economically weak, able to support her population only through export, Germany requires a passive currency policy. Any independent alteration in the currency would isolate her, and any isolation of Germany would be a satisfaction to her enemies, for it would mean the loss of markets.

The "cynics out of ethos" may rest content. There is no need for them to pursue any desperado policy, there is no need whatever for them to conduct Germany through the Slough of Despond, the international process of deflation brings despond enough.

CURRENCY AND DEBT SERVICE

Must the world, then, look on for ever with folded hands while France locks up gold in her vaults, and must it patiently put up with the sufferings which that country is bringing on it in its unfruitful greed?

Not necessarily. We said just now that gold is distinguished by nothing else but the extent of its acceptance.If Germany alone were to propose to go in for inflation, nothing would come of it but harm to herself. It would be quite a different matter if the world were to resolve on an international extension of the existing credit, perhaps by making use for credit purposes of the gold reserves at present unused in the world. That would not in any way be an inflation of currency, but simply an expansion of credit, or, rather, a remobilization, in order to make credit mobile again in the principal place where at present it is frozen fast, in Germany's short-term obligations. This is virtually the line of action indicated in the valuable proposals of the German Schmitz and the Belgian Francqui.

Quite certainly these proposals should serve to set world trade in motion once more for a period, so that the German car, at present stuck fast, could once more proceed with the rest. There would, it is true, be no change in the steady trend of the whole journey, the fundamental cause of trouble, the indebtedness, would remain the same, if it would not actually be in some degree accentuated. Nevertheless, movement is everything and immobility is death. These proposals are, in any case, thought out on the basis of world trade, and they are not, like the inflation proposals of the German extremists, based on crude misconceptions.

What is the good of it all if the proposals are wrecked by French opposition? Will not France oppose any change which would set a time limit, however remote, to the power which her gold holdings give her on the Continent? Schmitz anticipated in his proposal, which is the ablest of all, that an interest of two per cent would need to be provided for the stocks of gold, at present lying idle, which would be mobilized as cover through the B.I.S. Judging from the fate of the Norman Plan, it is doubtful whether France would agree.

But possibly she would be more accessible with such a plan if tendencies increase in the money market which are the compulsory working out of the crisis and the logical consequence of France's gold policy, more or less its repetition in private shape. If this still had no effect, it is conceivable that these tendencies might increase to panic strength, until the whole theory of note banks reached the end of its wisdom and the day came when the strongest gold currency was endangered.

The following considerations go beyond the facts and are only intended to indicate possibilities. Who has still the courage to oppose possibilities with an "out of the question"? Who, only a few weeks ago, would have thought it possible that rich America, with the greatest gold reserve in the world, would ever get into a position in which she would have to defend her dollar?

The classic theory of deposit bank business proceeds from the assumption that the depositors will never all want simultaneously to withdraw their deposits, but only a few of them. Just as the classic theory of gold currency (not gold nucleus currency) proceeds from the assumption that all the bank-notes will never be simultaneously presented for payment in gold.

This assumption is a pure assumption of a probability, just as every phenomenon of the market is a matter of probability. If the improbable but quite possible event occurs that more depositors than the assumed fraction demand their deposits simultaneously, the bank must put up its shutters.

When this occurred in Germany, no one was greatly surprised, for it was well known that Germany had an extraordinary quantity of short-term debts abroad. Now the same fate has befallen the American provincial banks. Where is rich America's foreign indebtedness? What ever has happened?

The statement of the American Federal Reserve Bank gives the explanation. The total of payment media in circulation increased by a milliard dollars in the first nine months of 1931, by six hundred millions in the last three of these alone. It may be estimated that of the total payment media in circulation in October 1931, 5,430,000,000 dollars, one milliard is hoarded. The gold circulation alone increased 24,000,000 dollars between June and October, being 376,000,000 in the latter month. It is surprising that, often as rumour has credited it with doing so, the United States has not even yet stopped the free issue of gold, for every hoarded gold coin is equivalent to two and a half times its value in hoarded notes.—The complement of the note-hoarding is the reduction in deposits. The total deposits in the ten principal New York deposit banks fell from 8,160,000,000 dollars at the beginning of the year to 7,270,000,000 at the end of the third quarter.

Thus the American citizen is systematically at work turning his deposits into bank-notes. He no longer trusts his bank. How does he know whether it has not lost on sterling assets, whether it has not shares in its possession that have fallen, credits outstanding that are frozen fast? He means to have security.

There is money enough available for note-hoarding. The debt service sees to that. We know the sums that are liberated yearly by the debt service. What is the poor American capitalist to do with the money? He has tried everything: bought goods, bought shares, subscribed to foreign issues—everywhere he has lost. Amid the general decline, stability without interest is the best form of interest; accordingly he buys gold and gold-covered notes.

Already America is calculating with concern when her note circulation will reach the limit of the gold cover. And then?

If the gold cover of the dollar were brought in the slightest degree into question, the American capitalist would take refuge as quickly as he could in French francs or other notes with reliable gold cover. Already the note-hoarding has passed from America to Europe. In Switzerland the circulation of bank-notes was relatively stable; in 1929 the monthly average circulation amounted to 855,700,000 Swiss francs. In 1930 it rose to 894,000,000; in September 1931 it had risen to 1,395,000,000. The figures from Holland are exactly on a par with these. Thus the American State is itself providing its citizens, through the debt service, with the money with which to give it an adverse balance of international payments and to bring its currency into peril.

If France had dethroned the dollar, her victory would have brought her no enduring joy. For the corresponding process would have been repeated with the franc. The increase in the French note circulation has long been noticeable; up to now it has steadily been attributed simply to the hoarding instincts of the French *petit bourgeois*. That in a time of general shrinkage of trade and industry the bank-note might also become the "investment stock" of the big capitalist is a circumstance with which no one has yet reckoned. No one has considered the fact that when, in consequence of the enduring crisis, all other possibilities of investment fail, the debt service might exercise a pressure on the currency. The debt service has been the ruin of share capital; the next thing will be for it to gnaw at the gold cover of the currency and so at the currency itself.

The daily transports of gold show that these are no mere flights of fancy. If we are looking ahead in continuing the lines of the ascertainable curves, the direction of the curves is, for all that, already a reality.

All things economic find expression in one form or another in the reports of the note banks. Hitherto only Germany's impoverishment has found expression in them. It is certainly a good thing that the moneys of the debt service have enough at present to feed on in shares and other investment opportunities and are not directly applying themselves to the bank-notes. That is the last phase of the workings of the debt service, for there would then be no other object left for the liberated moneys. If the general "crisis of confidence," or, to put it more simply, anxiety, has become acute enough, the sharpest raising of the discount rate will be impotent to prevent note-hoarding. Then no rate of interest will be too high to pay for security.

France has seen the danger ahead in good time. During the discussions in Washington her main concern was patent—to end the rivalry of franc and dollar and to increase the gold cover by making it more or less a common cover. America sacrificed her past discount policy to the achievement of unison. With heroic endurance she had held to the discount rate of one and a half per cent, until the risk of injury to herself had come, in order not to destroy the hope that cheap money might bring back a revival. Now France has carried her point of view; that means, in practice, that discount policy no longer serves to assist and stimulate credit, but only to maintain the defence of gold. Virtually the last hope is thus abandoned of the possibility of the crisis being overcome by the money market through its own mechanism.

If the Governments are thus, in their anxiety for the currencies, by their own act putting out of operation the mechanisms of self-healing in which the classical theory puts its faith, they should be all the more ready to recognize that it is impossible to go on with the present system of shifting of credit, that the whole system must be abandoned, and that a causal therapy must be introduced.

CAUSAL THERAPY

We will first consider the ideal therapy resulting from the recognition of the cause of the malady. Afterwards we shall examine how far this ideal therapy would meet the actual conditions that face us.

If our thesis is right, that the crisis is a working out of the disorders which have been set up by the service of the war indebtedness as a whole and are steadily continued in existence by it, it follows that the complete therapy would be the ending of the whole service of the war debts, external and internal alike.

Such a proposal looks utterly insane. It would mean demanding that the creditor States should overtly or tacitly embark on State bankruptcy. Would they, as victor States, ever agree to incur the odium of this? And would it not be at the same time the greatest of injustices towards the loan-holders, who years before had lent their money trustfully to the State?

Not so fast! We must not boggle at phrases. After all, the British action in letting the pound drop is equivalent in relation to the loan-holders to a thirty per cent bankruptcy, although Britain is a victor State.

An objector less ready to fly out in indignation will perhaps reply: "Certainly, if anyone has an infected lung, the 'ideal therapy' is, after all, to cut out the lung. All Procrustean cures are 'ideal' in type, and the only question is whether the patient will survive them. If tomorrow all the American, British, and

French war loans lying in the safes of the banks were declared valueless, trade and industry would indeed be entirely bankrupt."

But we are considering the ideal case only in order to see where we stand. We have no intention whatever of cutting out the whole lung, we only want to know where to apply the knife.

Let us consider what would happen if on and after tomorrow all payments on account of war-debt obligations, external and internal, were temporarily suspended. To begin with, the State budgets of the creditor States would be reduced by about forty per cent. Taxes and duties would be correspondingly lightened, the masses would quickly begin to buy again after the deprivations of recent years, and trade would with certainty enjoy the longed-for revival.

"And over-production? And rationalization? And the surplus from the harvests?"—The errors that have been committed in the last five years in one-sided extension of productive capacity can certainly not be made good in a day. But at least a beginning would have been made in enabling consumption slowly to grow up towards the new scale of production, whereas at present it is shrinking more and more below the volume of production.

"But the cessation of the incomes from loan interest? The credits built up on the loan paper and now themselves in trouble?"—To begin with, the cessation of the loan-interest payments would have the beneficent effect of bringing the hoarded notes back into circulation. The note banks would feel the relief. However, apart from that—we in Germany have survived the collapse of the inflation flotations in Germany after the German war loans had become valueless, and today we have that collapse entered in our books as a process of recovery. Probably the losses that would be incurred in the creditor countries would very soon be overtopped by the gains of the newly revived trade. That is no mere surmise, but is as certain as it is that today the losses in the crisis through the decline in purchasing power many times exceed the amounts of the war-debt service, high as those are.

For the moment, however, our therapy is mainly a tentative consideration, to determine the quarter in which the possibility of escape lies. It will not seriously be suggested by anyone that there should be a sudden debasement of the war loans. So abrupt a shifting of values would in any case be bound to produce a shock, in whatever direction it were to take place.

Our proposal can only make an impression if we first show its integral effect. It becomes then an executive question how to transfer it to the field of differentials.

Let us consider the matter as an entirely concrete proposition: let us assume that we had the opportunity of turning over the whole apparatus of world trade as it stands to a competent business man, with instructions to make an entirely fresh beginning and draw up, with a perfectly free hand, an opening balance free from any debt entry. No business man of any capacity would doubt that it is possible to make this magnificently organized undertaking work at a profit. For everything is in excellent condition: the apparatus of production is better intact than ever, the technique of the distribution of goods is incomparably more rapid than ever before, the organization of credit is more perfect than ever, never before have men had a finer apparatus at their service. In the apparatus itself there is not the slightest trace of ill health, the malady is confined to the books. If from tomorrow onwards we had only to find interest on the productively employed capital, the world would be well there and then, in spite of all rationalization and the like.

What is the use of these fine thoughts, if they are built up on a supposition that can never be realized?

But if we admit that the only sure remedy is unattainable, must we not there and then abandon all hope?

CAPITALISM AT THE CROSS-ROADS

Never let us indulge the illusion that America will make us a free gift of our Reparation debts out of pure love for us Teutons—for all that she is asked to do so almost every day in the German newspapers. Nor is it ever to be expected that the American holders of war-loan stock, impressed by what has been adduced in this book, will light a great bonfire and throw their war-loan paper into it.

The only remaining hope of escape lies in the world being induced to consider what course offers the better business results or the lesser loss.

The creditor half of humanity is faced inexorably with the choice between two alternatives—whether it shall lose the capital which it has invested in public loans or the capital which it has invested in private productive enterprise. If the world of creditors insists that the loan paper shall be maintained at its existing level, and that, accordingly, production shall continue to be burdened with taxation liabilities which make it impossible for it to be carried on at a profit, restriction of production must continue further, firms must continue to go into liquidation, and the index number of share prices will continue to fall.

If that were all, it would be possible to say: "Since money has got to be lost, it makes no difference, after all, whether it is lost on stocks or shares. Public loan securities are not kept lying idle in the safe, but are used as the basis of credit in other directions. (Even if not to the same extent in the U. S. A. as in Germany.) What does it matter which holdings show the loss?"

But that is not the whole story. The money that comes in by way of interest and amortisation is mostly sent, as experience shows, back to the capital market for reinvestment; consequently losses on stock holdings mean reductions in the formation of new capital. Losses of productive capital mean the closing down of works, unemployment, and falling prices in the world market. The consequence is that losses of share capital, owing to its special nature, have manifold repercussions. Will the world see this and draw its conclusion?

At the moment the creditor section of humanity is very far from having reached the point of realizing that further capital has got to be written off the world's books.

This bitter fact can be made plain to it also in the following way:

To say that in the World War expenditure amounting to a million million or seven hundred thousand million gold marks was paid out is in the last resort absurd, since there simply is not so much money in the world. Germany showed how this game of expenditure could have been carried on into millions of millions—and it is probable that it would have been carried on, had not hunger interposed itself on one side as the ultimate reality which cannot be disposed of by any multiplication. To show where the limit lies up to which a nation's wealth may justifiably be mobilized by means of credits would lead to complicated considerations; in any case, the limit lies far below the nominal amount of the world's internal debts. America imagines that, as her dollar stands at its full value, her war loans also stand at full value, since they stand in dollars, and that they are fully mobilizable. Although the dollar is good, the loans will not be capable of liquidation and amortisation at their full amount, or at most only in the course of a period so long that the increase in the national economic activities comes to its aid. A public debt can be inflated, even if the currency is at full value. This simple circumstance has not yet been generally realized. In the first years after the War the inflatedness of the war debt was not realized because it quietly went on with its paper existence and only relatively small amounts were set free through interest payments. The greater, however, the amount which this unfruitful debt produced in interest, through a falsified productivity, and cast into the economic system, and the greater the amount which it withdrew at another point from the economic system, the more severely was the pressure of the inflated public debt felt.

Every German business man has been through the moment when he had to abandon all calculating on the basis of his pre-war capital and face his new position on the strength of the assets that still remained to him. The Governments of the creditor States have not yet proceeded to that painful stock-taking and are still a long way from it at present. They are convulsively clinging to the illusion of the actual existence in the world of the assets that they have down in their books as loan dues. As the American war loans are quoted above par on the New York Stock Exchange, the private capitalist of the creditor countries is also prevented from proceeding in his turn to the said painful stock-taking. We must bear clearly in mind in Germany that the trade and industry of the creditor countries are at present in the condition in which ours would be if all the assets formed through the taking up of the German war loans were still maintained in our books at their nominal value. The eliminating effects of the deflation period that all of us have experienced as a process of recovery have not yet been experienced by the economic systems of the creditor States. The world crisis is the slow and very oppressive process of the making up of the arrears of that deflation.

CONVERSION

Britain has gone off gold. If the pound has fallen some thirty per cent, that means that the Birtish State debt has been reduced by thirty per cent. If Britain were ever to propose to raise the pound again to its old level, she would have to raise the loan debt correspondingly. That she is scarcely likely to be able to do. She will probably return to gold only at something below par; that will mean in effect that she has correspondingly reduced her debt by conversion. It might be asked why Britain did not proceed directly to conversion, for conversion is no new thing in budgetary legislation. Since June 30, 1929 the five per cent British war loan has been redeemable at par; at one time it was very dear, for, being tax-free, its interest rate is equivalent to five and a half per cent. Its conversion has been under discussion for a long time, though only to five or four and a half per cent. Probably the fact that a considerable amount of the loan stock is held abroad was felt to be a difficulty, and fear was felt that, if the conversion was not very carefully prepared for, the pound would be endangered. It was desired to await the most favourable moment, until the time came when by going off the gold standard the creditors had to be faced with an involuntary conversion.

America should learn from this. There is certainly no present menace to the quotation of the American loans. But if America allows world trade to collapse, she will have to find the whole of the interest and amortisation for her debt, to the last cent, from her own resources, and that will be beyond even America's strength. America is aware of that, and in 1930 she secured Congressional authority for a conversion to the extent of ten milliard dollars. The first of the maturity dates is June 1932, when 1,900,000,000 dollars of the 3.5 per cent Liberty Loan becomes repayable. Of the fourth (4.25 per cent) Liberty Loan, 6,300,000,000 dollars will mature in October 1933.

The leading stocks in the Wall Street list went above par long ago and bring in a return of barely 3 per cent. The 800,000,000-dollar 3⅛ per cent loan which America recently issued for the consolidation of short-term debts was over-subscribed, it will be remembered, seven times over. If, as seems practicable after this test, the American war loans were converted to the level of 3 per cent, the interest service would be diminished by some hundred million dollars, or nearly half of the sum that America has to claim under the Young Plan out of the Reparation payments. This cut in the debts, and the corresponding reduction of Reparation burdens, would thus already be possible through a transaction in the open market, without anything being done that would be in conflict with the capitalist economic system.

Up to now, not only has no such conversion been effected, but just the opposite has happened. Through the rise in the value of gold the effective value of the debts has been given an unobserved upward conversion. As prices have fallen and the purchasing power of the dollar has risen, the loan-holder now receives back considerably more than he lent during the war. This circumstance makes it possible, in the name of moral justice, for the State to undertake a conversion of quite different dimensions. No one can answer to the masses who are suffering from economic distress for the loan creditors being now paid back by the State, in effect, more than they lent. According to Fisher, the American index number of wholesale prices, under the new calculation which takes the price level of 1926 as 100, had fallen in July 1931 to 69.8. In 1917 the prices were some 12 per cent and in 1918 20 per cent higher than in 1926. On the basis of the fall in wholesale prices, therefore, it would be thoroughly justifiable to reduce the capital amount of the loans in the ratio of 3 to 2. We will be moderate, and content ourselves with a reduction in the ratio of 5 to 4. That would be a diminution of 20 per cent, only two thirds of what the British loan creditors have now lost through the fall in sterling, and in any case a smaller reduction than that of wholesale prices. That reduction of capital value would bring the American loan debt down from its present figure of 16,000,000,000 gold marks to 12,800,000,000; the interest service, for which (without amortisation) 640,000,000 dollars was expended in 1929–30, would be reduced to 512,000,000 dollars. That in itself would effect a saving of 128,000,000 dollars. Yet this conversion would only have balanced the difference between the purchasing power at the time of the issue and at present. It would, further, be an entirely just demand that these loan papers should be brought down to the present rate of interest on Government stocks; that is, converted downwards by an average of one per cent. That would further reduce the sum of 512,000,000 dollars to the sum of 384,000,000 dollars. The total saving in the interest service would thus be 256,000,000 dollars, almost as much as America receives from the Reparation remittances.

That, however, is not the only possibility of effecting a saving. One must ask oneself whether in the existing economic situation it is really justifiable that America should go on amortising at her past rate. We know how energetically America has pushed on with her amortisation since the end of the War, and the more the expenditure on the interest service falls through the reduction in the total of the loans, the more she raises the allocation to amortisation. For amortisation alone she paid out:

in 1925–6 .... 487,400,000 dollars
in 1926–7 .... 519,600,000 dollars
in 1927–8 .... 540,200,000 dollars
in 1928–9 .... 549,600,000 dollars
in 1929–30 .... 553,000,000 dollars

and the budget for 1930–1 provides for 635,300,000 dollars. Thus, the worse the economic situation becomes, the more money the United States is expending on amortisation. Meanwhile the loan-holders have no objection at all today if the State keeps their money, as the level of price quotations plainly shows. What could be more to their taste than for the State to administer their money? Is it really necessary, in view of the economic situation, to push on with the amortisation in this way?

The brief conclusion from these considerations is: America can with ease dispense with the whole of her receipts from the Reparation payments, if she converts her debts in correspondence with the decline in purchasing power and in the international rate of interest on Government stocks and slightly retards the tempo of her amortisation. This sacrifice costs the American taxpayer not a single cent.

But the foregoing survey shows this also: Should the opposition to a conversion of her internal indebtedness be too great, and should America be only ready as yet permanently to reduce the external indebtedness, she need not even convert. Since delay is dangerous, she can cheerfully dispense with all receipts from Reparations if she merely effects a big reduction in the allocation for amortisation. She need not even entirely suspend amortisation, there will still remain a substantial sum available for it. Nor does she run any danger of losing through repayment at maturity, as the level of price quotations shows. This operation also costs the American taxpayer not a single cent and does not even require special legislation, but could be carried through within the framework of the budget.

POSSIBILITIES?

Is there any possibility of making this proposal, which may have a naïve appearance in the eyes of the financial expert and yet rests on so strong a moral basis, so obvious to everybody that its realization would be conceivable?

To begin with, the proposal has the advantage that it is dependent exclusively on the American Government. For some time past it has been the fashion for every economic article to end with the sentence: "It is for the politicians to decide." Have we not by now had quite enough of politics? Is it not surely plain by now that every decision which is left to the politicians to take sooner or later gets silted up? If politics are to be our hope, then hope is in a bad way.

If it is true that the key to world trade lies today in America's hands, it must follow that America alone can bring help. And the fact that our plan could be realized by an American action entirely within the sphere of America's home politics is also evidence of its soundness.

But is there the slightest possibility of persuading American financial capital voluntarily to cut off a piece of its own flesh, through conversion, simply for the sake of world trade? If anything is worth the sacrifice, the maintenance of world trade is. The sacrifice would be equivalent to the lesser loss—that is, to the better business.

That it should be possible to find a Congressional majority for the compulsory conversion is beyond doubt, for the taxpayers are more numerous than the loan-holders. It would only depend on a party having an interest in developing the necessary propaganda for the conversion.

At bottom the Americans are very willing to work for an ideal when it is also good business. The World War was made popular among the Americans as a crusade against Prussian militarism, although they probably had never seen a Prussian soldier in uniform. Where is the ambitious American politician who will organize the crusade against the world crisis?

The plan has the further advantage that there is no need to consult France. For that also we should have learnt: anything that might bring a mitigation of the tension between the powers produced by the War tends to come to grief through French opposition. A devaluation of the American State loans is about the only thing against which France cannot well raise any objection, for the French capitalists have lost four fifths of their own loans. It was, of course, seen to in the Young Plan that no one but France should do well out of a reduction of the war debts.

In the direction indicated lies the last opportunity of producing a mitigation of the grave situation of world trade. If this path is not taken, world trade, in its instinctive effort to right itself, will produce other means of eliminating the superfluous loan capital. Either the productive private capital will be further brought down, so that reductions of capital and writings off will become necessary in quarters where it would never have been dreamed of, credits will have to be written off as bad debts which at present are cheerfully being continued as "frozen"; or else the same remedy will come into play that has already got rid of half of the war debts—the inflation of the currency. The events in Britain have brought an unexpected confirmation of this theory. Not that we wish to contend that the fall of sterling had to come of necessity—it could probably have come quite differently if provision had been made in time. We only want to draw attention to the point attacked—how it was possible that the crisis should have been able to attack the currency. Pure crises of production, in which category the present crisis is constantly being placed, set bank-notes free in consequence of business stagnancy and actually relieve the pressure on the note banks more than is welcome to them. It was no mere chance that the MacDonald Government fell owing to the impossibility of balancing the budget.

Whatever may be thought in detail of these proposals, one thing is incontrovertible: the mitigation of the crisis must proceed this time from the State budgets; that is, on the conditions which are necessary for the relief of the budgets; consequently, from the legislator, and the American legislator. The revival of purchasing power which is necessary for the ending of the depression must be effected by cuts in the State budgets under the heading "Public Debt Service." Industry alone cannot effect the revival.

If the Governments finally fail, and if trade and industry are left to themselves, the burden of the dead weight of indebtedness can only be thrown off by their rolling themselves up like a sick beast and shrinking, continually shrinking, until in the end the world falls apart into a multiplicity of reduced national economic systems. Then the protectionists of all countries will have their way, though not because there was no other way, but because the world had not the insight to enable it to pursue the other way. It will be poor comfort for impoverished humanity to know that it owes its sufferings to itself.

THESES

(Indication of contents, for hurried readers)

It is a test of clearness of thought if one can indicate the contents of a book in a few sentences.

1. Of the current explanations of the economic crisis, none is adequate, as is evident from the simple fact of the disagreement of the economists. (Conscientious economists—for instance, Wagemann—admit that the cause of the crisis is unknown.) In particular, the attribution of it, so frequently made, to rationalization affords no final explanation, but itself requires to be carried further back—otherwise the disgrace of the "ill-judged outlay" would be too great.

2. The contention so often made on the German side, that the main cause of the upsetting of economic equilibrium lies in the Reparation payments, fails to explain how a sum so small as these payments are in comparison with the amount of the world turnover could produce many times its own amount in losses through the crisis; and is, in consequence, justly viewed abroad with distrust.

3. In order to answer the question whether there is any intrinsic connexion between political debts and world crisis or only a "chance" coincidence in

time, it is necessary to take into consideration not only the external payment obligations, but the whole of the indebtedness arising from the War, the external, that is, and also the internal indebtedness. If the effect of the war obligations lay merely in the transfer of purchasing power from State to State, the receiving State would simply acquire as much additional purchasing power as the paying State lost; in other words, the net amount of world trade would remain constant. That was what the victor States reckoned on. Where the reckoning went wrong, why it proved impossible to localize the crisis on the debtor States—that is the question.

4. From the point of view of the productive capital of the world, the loan debts left by the War are dead capital carried forward, the interest and amortisation of which have to be provided by the live productive capital, although they are balanced by no asset in the form of capital outlay or the like. The interest and amortisation of this dead weight of debt throws a burden in the form of taxes and duties on the goods turnover of world trade and industry in all its phases and makes it unremunerative, so that it is steadily slackening down. The amount of this dead weight works out on a summary estimate at 210,000,000,000 gold marks (as at the time of the outbreak of the crisis in 1929). A dead weight of such dimensions makes the losses in the crisis and the shrinkage of world trade intelligible.

5. The capital losses through the crisis are proc-

esses of elimination or reduction of capital, through which the economic system, by virtue of its mechanism of self-preservation, tries to bring the total amount of the capital on which it has to earn interest into consonance with the yield of production. Since, in consequence of the authority of the State, the amount of the war debt outstanding is inviolable, the reduction takes place under the head of the productive private capital. If nothing is done by the administrator of the debt account, the State, this process of elimination through the crisis (or "deflation") will continue until the interest-bearing capital standing in the books of the world economic system agrees in amount with the value of the actually employed productive capital.

6. The effect of the dead weight of war indebtedness is not confined to the burdening of production and consumption with taxes and duties. On the other side there is a corresponding excessive formation of new capital, due to the interest and amortisation of the debt service. Thus the world indebtedness has the further effect of throwing out of balance the formation of new capital, the regulation of which is a component part of the capitalist system, and consequently the new investment of capital. The consequences are capital export and "ill-judged capital outlay."

7. Thus rationalization and the capital investment for carrying it into effect, and the burdening of colonial countries with indebtedness, are themselves

secondary symptoms. The excessive pace of rationalization finds its explanation, from the point of view of the technique of business management, in the desperate effort to show a profit once more from costings overburdened by taxes through the reduction of the component costs of the wages of labour; or, from the point of view of the national economy, the effort to produce from the yield of productive capital the increased return which is required in order to pay the interest on the dead burden of debt.

8. Capitalist trade and industry can only be enabled to function freely once more if, as is imperatively required by the essential nature of capitalism, interest has only to be paid by the capital which is balanced by a corresponding real asset in the form of fixed or working capital. To demand interest on a capital sum unproductively expended, simply because it was lent out at interest and so, under the routine of private legality, is entitled to its interest, is the expression of an out-of-date *rentier* type of capitalism, entirely at variance with the fundamental nature of the type of capitalism that has conquered the world.

9. The decline in world prices (or the rise in the value of gold) has brought a corresponding rise in the intrinsic value of the American war loans. A conversion of the American Liberty Loans is thus morally entirely justified. If the American Government were to reduce these loans by conversion no more than twenty per cent—by an amount, that is, that falls

short considerably of the decline in world market prices—and if it would at the same time reduce the interest on them to a rate corresponding to the present world rate of interest on Government securities and would somewhat retard the present very drastic tempo of amortisation, it would be able to dispense permanently with all receipts from Reparation payments, without the American taxpayer having in consequence to bear the burden of a single cent more in taxes.

10. In any case, the overcoming of the present depression can only be effected through the State budgets, and consequently through the action of the legislators of the creditor countries, by making legislative provision for the reduction of the State budgets, which at present are unduly inflated. This reduction must be made under the heading of Public Debts. Only by a reduction under this head can the purchasing power be restored to the masses which is necessary for the revival of trade.

THE TWELFTH HOUR OF CAPITALISM

THE ECONOMIC AND POLITICAL SITUATION

FOREIGN BONDS
by Max Winkler

RUSSIA
by Hans von Eckardt

MONEY AND POLITICS ABROAD
by James Kerr Pollock

EUROPEAN ALLIANCES AND ALIGNMENTS
by William L. Langer

POWER ETHICS
by Jack Levin

TWENTY YEARS OF THE CHINESE REPUBLIC
by Harold Archer Van Dorn

A NOTE ON THE TYPE IN WHICH THIS BOOK IS SET

This book is set on the Linotype in Baskerville. The punches for this face were cut under the supervision of George W. Jones, the eminent English printer and the designer of Granjon and Estienne. Linotype Baskerville is a facsimile cutting from type cast from the original matrices of a face designed by John Baskerville, a writing master of Birmingham, for his own private press. The original face was the forerunner of the "modern" group of type faces, known today as Scotch, Bodoni, etc. After his death in 1775, Baskerville's punches and matrices were sold in France and were used to produce the sumptuous Kiel edition of Voltaire's works.

COMPOSED, PRINTED AND BOUND
BY VAIL-BALLOU PRESS, INC.,
BINGHAMTON, N. Y.
PAPER MADE BY
S. D. WARREN CO.,
BOSTON

For Product Safety Concerns and Information please contact our EU representative GPSR@taylorandfrancis.com
Taylor & Francis Verlag GmbH, Kaufingerstraße 24, 80331 München, Germany

www.ingramcontent.com/pod-product-compliance
Lightning Source LLC
LaVergne TN
LVHW011122300926
849160LV00008B/475

9780367245627